THE BLUEPRINT TO REVEALING

JESUS

1 Book - 30 Days - 1 Answer

An apologetics-based book tailored for mentorship to
uncover evidence for revealing the Divinity of Jesus

Dr. Jason H. Jackson

ISBN (10:0-9965867-2-5)
ISBN (13:978-09965867-2-6)

Dedication

I would first like to dedicate this book to Dr. Myles Munroe and John Paul Jackson, two great leaders who have left us with a beautiful imprint and torch to run with. Next, I would like to dedicate this book to the emerging leaders and stewards of the next, and possibly by God's design, greatest generations.

To my precious wife, Natalie, and to my outstanding children–Nalani, Jessica, and Joshua: You all respectively allot me the opportunity to serve as your husband and father. Natalie: You endure a heavy burden in my physical absences, but I am comforted in your understanding and participation in the assignment which was bestowed upon our family. We have many miles to go, but I am confident in God's ability to protect, nourish, and cover you and our children. I continue to pray the love that we have for each other is multiplied around the world. Since day one, you have been my angel, my rock, my fortress, and the token of my heart. I am proud to confess my love and admiration for you, which continues only to allow room for expanse.

To my best friend and mentee, C. Gino Piompino: Thank you for adhering to God's calling. Without you, the road would not have been as exciting. Surely, we have experienced tremendous seasons of mountains and valleys together. They have only strengthened our trust for one another. You are one of the finest, most transparent humans I know. The world will benefit from you greatly in your season.

To my beloved mother, Samdaye Johnson: I would not change one iota of our lives together. I come to respect, cherish, and love you more every day that I am alive.

To my father, John L. Jackson and my step-father, Glenn Williams: Thank you for recognizing and investing into my destiny at an early age.

To my Aunt Raj and Uncle Daryl: You were the first to show me a complete God-fearing family. Your influence has impacted many lives through my personal ministry. To my beloved Lion's Den Missions Base-Fort Lauderdale leadership team: Each of you are aligned with my calling which has allowed us to impact the lives of many–with countless more to go!

To my VFA-22 United States Navy family: *"Hooorah"!*

Finally and foremost, to my FATHER in Heaven: Though there were many times I felt alone, without human bonds and acceptance, YOU were there. I pray that I am always in position to receive your grace, mercy and love. Heavenly FATHER, my prayer is that this book will fulfill its purpose of accelerating Your desire for discipleship and relationship among Your people; *My prayer is not that you take them out of the world, but keep them in the world and that all Believers will be one in you.*

Table of Contents

Acknowledgements

Translating the content of this writing into tangible form has been nothing less than daunting and at many times frustrating. Whole-heartedly underwriting this book while actively participating in my 5-member family, charting the helm of our businesses, and spiritually fathering a newly planted ministerial hub has been one of the greatest challenges of my life. Nevertheless, I chose to emphasize upon the determination of leaving the wisdom God has conferred upon me to the next generation.

I am wholly convicted that this book is best served as a reliable tool which will provoke Christian maturation and establish a foundation for discipleship as well as apologetics—all while giving a reason for the hope we have. As Christians we should embrace constructive skepticism and use it as a barometer of our understanding. In fact, I consider myself a skeptic who at one point did not trust in the Bible's content. Years ago, I began a journey for answers. The material found in this book stems from my desire for certainty.

In the fullness of truth, I would not have embarked upon this journey had it not been for the love I have for my Lion's Den family. Week after week, I witnessed my flock love God with their whole hearts, although they did not truly apprehend the infallibility of The Word of God. In response, I was searching for an instrument that not only could provoke ripeness among my flock, but incite a cyclical pattern of discipleship and mentorship that would perpetuate in my absence. All in all, with the best the Lord could give through me, I present to you this tool. I am thankful to you and hope that you will share and utilize this book for its primary function. I pray you find clarity and truth at the end of your 30-Day journey. I look forward to hearing from you. My direct contact information can be found at the end of the book.

Preface

Navigating a World of Many Truths

In a world where political correctness has become paramount, the term "truth" is more fluid. The evolution of perceived truth has been fueled by our desire to embrace all ideologies, faiths, and moral frameworks as valid. All of which being done in an effort to avoid offense and to provide a perceived sense of inclusion to all. Therefore, in today's world it is fashionable to suggest that no availability should be made for a single set of definitive, or *absolute truths*. The argument pretenses truth being based upon what each person believes, according to their chosen lifestyle. This sort of truth is known as *relative truth*, meaning to some, *"It can be true for you, but not for me"*.

Having grown up in a biracial, bi-spiritual home when it was less embraced, I experienced firsthand what it was to receive two very passionate, yet very different points of view. Yet, could both sets of truths be absolute or was it all a matter of perspective? For example, my mother may have said that curry-based Indian food was the best. From her point of view, it was an accurate representation. However, not passing the test of truth, according to my father's taste buds, disqualified it from being an absolutely true statement. Though, the claim was undeniably true relative to my mother who held the preference.

In 2016, we have far more daunting truths to consider. Imagine a country in which the ruling government seeks to exterminate a racial minority because they believe the group poses the risk of ethnic contamination. Now imagine if the majority of non-minority citizens were to agree with the government's decision to kill the minority group, then begins efforts to take action. Do you believe the country is making a horrific decision? If so, what would be the angle of your message to persuade them to halt the initiative? Remember, if morality is relative, they are not committing an atrocity because their actions are acceptable relative to their own culture, community, and interests. Still, if killing an entire minority group is wrong, though the culture approves of it, a case for absolute truth must be presented and established as an alternative.

I understand that the scenario above may seem extreme. However, the fact is it is happening all around the world. My aim is not to place the world's pressures on your shoulders. Rather, to illustrate that everyone cannot be right, at the same time. Ultimately, you must read this book intending to identify and solidify the source of absolute truth for your life.

Introduction
To The Earth With Purpose As Foretold
Day 1

Day 1
Introduction
Establishing Purpose and Framework

Upon completion of this book you should be able to:

1. Understand the purpose of the life of Jesus Christ

2. Explain how Jesus fulfilled prophecies which were spoken millennia before His coming

3. Explain the provisions Jesus gave to His Believers who would follow in His wake

4. Uphold biblical foundations which are constantly bombarded by New Age influences and other un-doctrinal forms

5. Utilize this book as a foundation to mentor others pertaining to the infallibility of Jesus Christ and His provisions for those who believe.

Suggested use of this book:

1. Agnostics/ Atheists: This writing can be used to afford you with a centralized, easy-to-read framework for examination on the basis of belief in Jesus.

2. New Believers: This writing can be used to provide a solid foundation for the reason why the decision was made to follow Christ. Studying with a more seasoned Christian is suggested.

3. Pastors/Ministry Leaders: This writing can be deployed through discipleship and home groups as a method to create synergy that is grounded in Biblical truth.

4. Evangelists/Missionaries: This writing can be used to proctor an evangelistic/ apologetics training class by breaking down the content into bi-weekly or weekly sessions to establish participating teams. It may also be used for a 30-day discipleship program.

5. Mature Christians: This writing may be used to provide you with the basis needed to substantiate personal faith and to begin imparting the material to new Believers.

Why Apologetics Matters

We live in an age of rapid change and movement. Faddish trends appear one day and promptly disappear the next. Today, many discussions about spirituality would likely fall into this category. Large segments of the younger generation are growing apathetic toward the discussion of unbiased, self-fulfilling spirituality. The prevalence of New Age spiritualism has accounted for a shift in the way people see truth. Besides this shift affecting many areas of our country's culture, it has had a potent effect on Believers in Christ.

In the hearts of many Christians, there is no question whether the Bible is absolute truth. But when pressed, it is uncovered that most cannot explain why the Bible, as opposed to the Qur'an or the Book of Mormon, is the infallible Word of GOD? Consequently, one must appeal to evidence to determine this. It is improbable that most Christians would accept a Muslim's statement such as, "The Qur'an is alive and powerful and sharper than a two-edged sword". In kind, they would certainly demand evidence for such a claim.

Without evidence to establish one's claim to authority, there is no good reason to accept that authority; hence, the need for validating the Bible through apologetics. For those who are unfamiliar with my personal ministry, I must express that my suggested method of validity does not come through apologetics or intellectualism alone. Jesus told the non-believers that if they do not believe Him, to at least believe in the miracles He performed (John 14:24). I believe the kingdom of GOD comes not in speech alone, but in a powerful demonstration, through supernatural validation.

Hopefully, as you read along, you will adopt a similar mindset. If not, that is okay. Salvation is not based upon your belief in miracles as much as it is centered upon your belief in Jesus. Remember, if you're going to illustrate the Gospel of Jesus predominantly through articulating historical facts, do it with love and compassion. I am concerned with an arising element of Christians who seem to yield biblical truths to prove themselves, rather than Christ. I implore you to do all things with love and by the leading of GOD'S Spirit.

Reliability of the Bible

Although I cannot expound greatly in this book, I wish to give you confidence in the accuracy of the Bible; particularly considering it will be at the center of our study. By comparing the places and events in the Bible to actual physical evidence we can demonstrate the truthfulness of the Bible as it relates to historical matters. Demonstrating the Bible's accuracy on historical events is not intended to prove the

Bible's correctness on spiritual matters. It dismisses the critic's claims about the Bible not being "true". If the Bible is true on historical events, then it is certainly worth examining.

For instance, Cyrus the Great was both a biblical and historical person. The Bible tells us after the defeat of Babylon by the combined Median-Persian Empire, Cyrus made a proclamation permitting the people of Judah to return home and to rebuild the Temple (2 Chron 36:22-23). This event in the Bible can be validated through historical Persian documents. The *Cyrus Cylinder* gives us the declaration from Cyrus himself. In fact, we can go to his tomb to validate his history. This same claim cannot be made for many other holy books.

When we affirm the perfect historical accuracy of the Bible, we are not claiming that our favorite English version, or even our best Hebrew text, is infallible. Our claim is only that the original manuscripts were without error. Though minimal by comparative historical standards, common errors have occurred in the *translation* and *transliteration* process (more or less depending upon the version that you choose). Still, you can rest assured knowing the Bible is the foremost authority as it relates to historical records.

Ultimately, there will be many skeptics who will passionately refute the accuracy of the Bible. As such, I make the following statement to you. *Your foundational belief in Christ cannot be centered upon what you have read, rather what you have experienced.* Your personal experience with Jesus Christ must be at the center of your trust in Him. All other evidence which support His claims should simply serve as a bonus.

Structuring The Gospel of Jesus in 4 Parts

How would you define the Gospel of Jesus? The Gospel, or Good News, of Jesus Christ is the cornerstone of Christian faith. However, due to the acceptance of *relative truth*, the perceived definition of the Gospel of Jesus has taken on many forms. Some Believers say that Jesus was GOD; others disagree. Some say that healing and prophecy still exist, yet others disagree. Some say that Jesus fulfilled the covenants of the Torah through His works, while again, others disagree. Considering the many means of thought surrounding the Gospel, I was inspired by GOD to break down the Good News of Jesus into four distinct parts. In doing so, this book will allow you to investigate the key areas of the Gospel often challenged by Believers and non-Believers alike.   Just remember this to access the full Gospel of Jesus Christ: (1)e Came, (2)He Went, (3)He Came, and (4) He Went.

1) *He Came* to Earth as foretold by GOD through HIS holy prophets. Jesus was not merely a man that *coincidentally* appeared. His birth and purpose was pre-announced so we could clearly identify Him as our promised Savior.

2) *He Went* to be flogged and crucified for our iniquities, sin, and sickness. Jesus took on the pains of the world providing us access to restorative life in adversity.

3) *He Came* back from the dead and rose the very same physical body that was torn and crucified. Jesus defeated death so you would not have to taste it if you believe.

4) *He Went* to heaven so GOD could give us the Holy Spirit. Jesus left us with His nature, character and power in the form of The Holy Spirt so we could continue His mandate to spread the Gospel within the same manner He did.

Questions for the Heart

Your answers to these questions are not meant to be criticized; rather, they should be analyzed. Use this section to get a gauge of where your current knowledge and heart are by answering honestly. Be sure to write each answer on your notepad.

1) What provoked you to begin this 30 day process to revealing Jesus?

2) Do you believe in the accuracy of the Bible? If so, why?

3) What are your 3 biggest questions about the life and purpose of Jesus?

4) What is your definition of the Gospel of Jesus Christ?

5) If the evidence in this book reflects the authentically divine nature of Jesus Christ, what will you do to seek a deeper personal relationship with Him?

Chapter 1: He Came
To The Earth With Purpose As Foretold
Days 2-7

Today, many non-Christian philosophers assert that Jesus was not a supernatural human being, deity, or GOD incarnate. Rather, their views of Jesus are restricted to the basic belief that He existed and was a good man who cared for many. Many orthodox Jewish followers agree with this sentiment, and at best, place Jesus as a well-known, progressive Jewish prophet.

Unfortunately, depending on your outlook, these assertions of Jesus cannot be true. Either Jesus is who He says He is, or He is a complete heretic. Jesus made sure there would be no middle ground regarding His nature and purpose by making major representations about His exclusive relationship with GOD and His ability to act on behalf of GOD. It was this rhetoric, which caused Jesus to be condemned and, ultimately, put to death by His peers.

It is important to note that the birth and mission of Jesus was established and prophetically recorded long before His arrival. There were no legitimate recorded prophecies foretelling details regarding the birth of other prominent religious leaders. There were no special predictions to alert the world of the coming of Muhammad (Islam), Joseph Smith (Mormonism), David Koresh (Branch Davidians), Charles Taze Russell (Jehovah's Witnesses), Siddhartha Gautama (Buddhism), or any other founder of the world's well known religions.

In this Chapter, you will learn that the Tanach (Old Testament), pinpointed numerous details about the life of Jesus and His purpose. Prudently scrutinize the details of each Study Scripture to determine if you believe Jesus unintentionally negotiated His way through life, or if He understood His unique assignment as Savior of the world. Finally, consider the statistical possibilities of Jesus fulfilling each of these prophecies.

Questions for the Heart

Your answers to these questions are not mean to be criticized; rather, they should be analyzed. Use this section to get a gauge of where your current knowledge set and heart are by answering honestly. Be sure to write each answer on your notepad.

1) Who do you believe Jesus was?

2) In your opinion, who did Jesus believe that He was?

3) Do you believe Jesus fulfilled prophecies? If so, which ones?

4) Who do you believe the disciples of Jesus thought He was?

5) Why did Jesus have such a strong following after a mere three years of ministry? Was it based upon who people expected Him to be?

The Ten Learning Steps

The Ten Learning Steps have been provided as a guide to help you make the most of each Study Scripture. Carefully focus on each Learning Step throughout this chapter to make the most of this endeavor.

For those who are willing, pray to GOD-in the name of Jesus- for HIS Truth to be revealed in you

Carefully read the Study Scripture at least 3 times, focusing on each minute detail.

Locate (online or hard copy) the Study Scripture in an amplified Bible to discover theparticulars of its content.

On a dedicated notepad, transcribe important thoughts derived from your initial glance.

Ensure to notate portions of the Study Scripture which have the greatest relevance to you.

Do your best to answer the Investigative Questions section without referencing the Study Scripture.

Check or complete the Investigative Questions section by using the corresponding Study Scripture.

Record findings, questions and additions to your dedicated notepad.

Insert the location of each Study Scripture in your phone, tablet or notepad for fuurereference and memorization.

If possible, discuss your questions and comments with spiritual leaders, mentors or friends who can guide you through this study.

As led, pray for clarity regarding areas of apprehension and ask GOD for deeper understanding.

Study Scripture: Genesis 3: 8-15 (CEB)

"8 During that day's cool evening breeze, they heard the sound of the Lord GOD walking in the garden; and the man and his wife hid themselves from the Lord GOD in the middle of the garden's trees. 9 The Lord GOD called to the man and said to him, "Where are you?"10 The man replied, "I heard your sound in the garden; I was afraid because I was naked, and I hid myself."11 He said, "Who told you that you were naked? Did you eat from the tree, which I commanded you not to eat?"
12 The man said, "The woman you gave me, she gave me some fruit from the tree, and I ate."13 The Lord GOD said to the woman, "What have you done?!"
And the woman said, "The snake tricked me, and I ate."
14 The Lord GOD said to the serpent, "Because you have done this cursed are you above all livestock and above all beasts of the field; on your belly you shall go, and dust you shall eat all the days of your life. 15 I will put enmity between you and the woman, and between your offspring and her offspring he shall bruise your head, and you shall bruise his heel."

Shedding Light on Genesis 3

Genesis is also known as the book of beginnings. For Bible believing Christians, Muslims, and Jews, it contains the foundation for all the dealings of the world- including principles of the relationship between GOD and man. while anticipating all future revelations of GOD. Considering its relative ambiguity for those beginning in or considering the Christian faith, I'd prefer not to start our investigation into the life of Christ with this verse. However, this is chronologically the first prophecy of the coming of Jesus recognized by most Christians.

Throughout the Blueprint for Revealing Jesus, you will find an abundance of clear evidence reflecting the divine nature of Jesus. Hopefully by the end of this book, your belief in Jesus would have been established or elevated to greater maturity. Thus, ultimately, allowing you to have taken on the spiritual understanding needed to receive the power found in the Study Scripture.

When readers first come in to contact with the Study Scripture, one question that always arises is, "What is the deal with the serpent?". Understandably so. If you are struggling with this notion, I suggest you consider it as an allegory for the time being. However, I would encourage those of faith to accept the scenario as literal. Either way, let us stay on topic and accept this verse as prophetically significant regarding the coming and purpose of Christ.

Prior to the Study Scripture, Adam and Eve walked the beautiful Garden of Eden in power and authority. They were given rulership over all animals and plant life. They did not have to farm because Earth produced vegetation according to their needs. There was no sickness, death, or even a need for bodily covering. Adam and Eve both walked with GOD and had face to face relationship with Him- as was HIS desire. In the Study Scripture, GOD is forced to uphold HIS laws towards Adam and Eve. However, HE didn't leave them without the hope of heaven.

Investigative Questions

1. What was GOD's reaction to the serpent? What does GOD's reaction tell you about HIS original desire for Adam and Eve? (v. 14)

_____

_____

_____

_____

_____

_____

_____

_____

_____

2. What did the Study Scripture say GOD would put between the woman and the serpent? How would you describe the new relationship between the woman and the serpent? (v. 15)

_____
_____
_____
_____
_____
_____
_____
_____
_____
_____

3. The Study Scripture mentions that the offspring of the woman and the serpent would be at odds, foretelling the prolonged battle against good and evil. How do you see the battle between good and evil playing out in the world today?

_____
_____
_____
_____
_____
_____
_____
_____
_____
_____
_____

4. GOD said the woman's male offspring would not just be an ordinary man, but that He would have the power to do what to the serpent? (vs. 15)

_____
_____
_____

_____
_____
_____
_____
_____
_____

5. The Study Scripture is symbolic and prophetic containing veiled messages. Assuming the seed of the woman to come is Jesus, why would GOD decide to announce His coming at this time? What did the serpent take from Adam and Eve (Read Genesis Chapters 2 and 3)?

_____
_____
_____
_____
_____
_____
_____
_____
_____
_____
_____

6. If GOD created man for relationship with HIM, would it be fair if HE forced the relationship? Should all relationships be established upon choice? How does having two trees in the garden provide free will to Adam and Eve?

_____
_____
_____
_____
_____
_____
_____
_____

Study Scripture: Micah 5:2

"2 But you, O Bethlehem Ephrathah, who are too little to be among the clans of Judah, from you shall come forth for me one who is to be ruler in Israel, whose coming forth is from of old, from ancient days."

Shedding Light on Micah 5

To keep the promise pure, GOD would need a remnant. He would need a GOD-seeking line of people who would believe in HIS promise of restoration (mentioned to Adam and Eve in Genesis 3:15) and be willing to fight to become the channel for the "Seed of the woman", or Eve's descendent. Therefore, in the lineage of The Seed we will see how GOD protected the promise HE made to Eve by eliminating billions of prospects so that we would have certainty in our search for the Savior.

This line of prophetic truth regarding the birth of the "Seed of the woman" or "Savior" becomes more and more miraculous as we become more aware of the details. Throughout the Study Scriptures, we will see how GOD identifies The Seed and fulfills HIS promises to Adam and Eve, Abraham, and others in spite of the continued opposition of the serpent. The road signs provided in this Chapter will enable you to pinpoint with great accuracy, who this Savior was. There will also be signs of when, where, and how He would be born. We will also discover other amazing details foretold by the Scriptures hundreds of years in advance.

The uniqueness of Jesus must be corroborated through prevailing prophecies. Validation of Jesus' fulfillment of prophecy would provide evidence demonstrating that He is not simply another of the world's great religious leaders. Instead, it would substantiate that He is the "Promised Seed" and answer to mankind's need of reconciliation with GOD. Pay close attention to every detail in each Study Scripture to determine your belief of Jesus' qualification as the "Promised Seed" and "Chosen Savior".

Investigative Questions

1. What city did GOD say through the Prophet Micah that a new ruler would be born? (v. 2)

_____
_____
_____
_____
_____
_____
_____
_____
_____

2. Read Matthew 2:4-6. What verse is quoted by the Jewish leaders when responding to King Herod?

_____
_____
_____
_____
_____
_____
_____
_____
_____
_____
_____

3. Where and when does the scripture say the new ruler would come from? (v. 2)

_____
_____
_____
_____
_____

_____

_____

_____

_____

_____

_____

_____

_____

4. Read a quote from Jesus in John 17:5. What did Jesus suggest regarding the timing of which He and His Father came into relationship? How does this correlate with the Study Scripture?

_____

_____

_____

_____

_____

_____

_____

_____

_____

_____

_____

5. Read Colossians 1:16-17 and John 1:1-3. What did Paul (the writer of Colossians) and John (Disciple of Jesus) think about the nature and possible pre-existence of Jesus? How does this correlate with answers to questions #3 and #4?

_____

_____

_____

_____

_____

_____

_____

_____

Day 5
The Lineage of Jesus Specified

Study Scripture: Genesis 49:8-10 *CEB*

"⁸Judah, you are the one your brothers will honor;
your hand will be on the neck of your enemies;
your father's sons will bow down to you.
⁹Judah is a lion's cub;
from the prey, my son, you rise up.
He lies down and crouches like a lion;
like a lioness—who dares disturb him?
¹⁰The scepter won't depart from Judah,
nor the ruler's staff from among his banners.
Gifts will be brought to him; people will obey him."

Shedding Light on Genesis 49

The entire Study Scripture reflects a prophecy from Jacob, a patriarch, who was the son of Isaac and the grandson of Abraham. After a monumental encounter with GOD, Jacob's name was changed to Israel. While on his death bed, Jacob called his sons together counseling them not to mingle with the Egyptians. He advised them to remain separate apart and together. Jacob declared GOD's purpose and vision as revealed to him by the Holy Spirit and thoughtfully dictated it to them. In the process of Jacob pronouncing blessings on each of his sons, he narrows the line to the tribe of Judah. This prophecy is not merely providing regard for Jacob's sons. Rather, it is describing the future of the people Israel. In this prophecy, GOD not only narrows the field, but broadens expectations to look for the One who will one day become ruler of Israel-GOD's chosen land.

Genesis 49 clearly states that out of the sons of Jacob, a royal line would arise to rule in Israel and, ultimately, over the world through the Savior to come. Additionally, the Study Scripture references the right to rule would remain within the Tribe of Judah and that out of Israel-which was a separate state-no one would assume the throne of Israel. This would not occur until Shiloh, the Peacemaker, was to come to rule and his kingdom be established. The term *Shiloh* is mentioned 33 times in the Torah (Old Testament).

In verse 10, we find the reference to Shiloh and His future coming. This obscure word is variously interpreted to mean "the sent" (John 17:3), "the seed" (Isaiah 11:1), the "peaceable or prosperous one" (Ephesians 2:14), which is, the Messiah. Prior to Shiloh's coming, the tribe of Judah would continue to maintain power and strength, signified by the scepter—the symbol of authority and rule of law.

Jacob blessed and prophetically declared over every one of his sons according to the will of GOD. For this study, we are focused on Jacob's son Judah. You are, however, strongly encouraged to read about the other messages Jacob gave to his other sons. After Jacob finished delivering his blessings, he prepared himself for transition into the Hand of GOD.

Investigative Questions

1. Who did Jacob say will be praised by their brothers (See Gen. 49:8)? (v. 8)

_____
_____
_____
_____
_____
_____
_____
_____
_____
_____
_____

2. In verse 8 of the Study Scripture, Jacob said, *"your hand shall be on the neck of your enemies"*. What did he mean? Read Psalm 18:40 and explain how this prophecy begins fulfillment (also refer to Gen. 49:4)?

_____
_____
_____
_____
_____
_____
_____
_____

3. Several decades after Jacob's prophecy, the book of Judges 1 reveals that after Joshua died, a group was sent to take the remaining land of Canaan. This is also known as modern day Israel. What group seized the remaining land? Why is that significant to the Study Scripture?

_____

_____

_____

_____

_____

_____

_____

4. Jacob prophesied in Genesis 49:10 that the "scepter", or kingship, would go to the tribe of Judah. Ultimately, this happens through King David. This was hundreds of years prior to the prophecy's fulfillment. Are David and Jesus related, if so how (See Matthew 1:1-17) ?

_____

_____

_____

_____

_____

_____

_____

_____

_____

5. In your opinion, if Jesus is to be the mentioned Savior, why is it important that He be born into the tribe prophesied of by Jacob? Could Jesus control what family He was born into if He was only a mere man?

_____

_____

_____

_____

_____

Day 6
The Virgin Birth of Jesus Foretold

Study Scripture: Isaiah 7:13-16 ESV

"13 And he said, "Hear then, O house of David! Is it too little for you to weary men, that you weary my GOD also? 14 Therefore the Lord himself will give you a sign. Behold, the virgin shall conceive and bear a son, and shall call his name Emmanuel.15He shall eat curds and honey when he knows how to refuse the evil and choose the good. 16For before the boy knows how to refuse the evil and choose the good, the land whose two kings you dread will be deserted."

Shedding Light on Isaiah 7

In the Study Scripture, Isaiah prophetically announces the birth of a magnificent child through a virgin to the house of David. Though this will not be a detailed explanation of this passage, I want to emphasize a few important points. The first point is there was a promise and judgment on the house of David (Isaiah 7:14). Notice this section was addressed to the whole house of David and not to just Ahaz or the immediate situation. It becomes both a promise to the house of David and a judgment. First, by the sign and promise of Isaiah 7:14, GOD is assuring the house of David that the alliance of Syria and Israel would not come to pass (Isaiah 7:1-2). GOD clarifies that no impersonator would ever sit on the throne of David.

The promise of the virgin birth was GOD'S response to the fallen line of David which had spiritually degenerated. GOD arranged for a replacement by One who would not fall in disgrace, yet still qualify to uphold the royal line of David. GOD would set aside the physical line of the merely human house of David, which would become even more corrupt during the reigns of the following kings.

In Hebrew, the word for virgin is "alma", which means "a mature, young, unmarried, and pure woman". Furthermore, the word "alma" is fully embraced for representing a young woman, one whose clear distinction is virginity. There is no Hebraic instance where "alma" designated a young woman who was not also a virgin. In this way, for one to be born of an "alma", a true miracle work of GOD must occur.

For clarity, belief in the virgin birth, supernatural healing, or speaking in supernatural languages qualifies or denies someone access to heaven. Your access to heaven is granted by responding in agreement to the gentle tug on your heart that Jesus is the way to heaven. From there , it is making the proper steps to follow Him. This is salvation at its basic form. The primary purpose of seeking truth in the virgin birth is to validate that Jesus fulfilled the requirements to be the Savior.

Investigative Questions

1. In Isaiah 7:13-14, GOD is speaking prophetically through the Prophet Isaiah to the House of David, The Tribe of Judah, telling them to take courage because a sign is coming. Who was responsible for giving the sign according to the text?

_____
_____
_____
_____
_____
_____
_____
_____
_____
_____
_____
_____
_____
_____

2. What was the sign to the house of David (Isaiah 7:14)?

_____
_____
_____
_____
_____
_____
_____
_____

3. What does the name *Emmanuel* mean? If possible, refer to Strong's Concordance to locate a definition.

_____
_____

_____
_____
_____
_____
_____
_____
_____
_____
_____

4. Read Isaiah 9:6 and Micah 5:2. How do these scriptures support the purpose of the name *Emmanuel*?

_____
_____
_____
_____
_____
_____
_____
_____
_____
_____
_____
_____

5. According to the Study Scripture (v.16), when will this miracle child know the difference between good and evil?

_____
_____
_____
_____
_____
_____
_____
_____
_____
_____

Study Scripture: Daniel 9:24-27

[24] "Seventy weeks have been decreed for your people and your holy city, to finish the transgression, to make an end of sin, to make atonement for iniquity, to bring in everlasting righteousness, to seal up vision and prophecy, and to anoint the most holy place. [25] "So you are to know and discern that from the issuing of a decree to restore and rebuild Jerusalem until Messiah the Prince there will be seven weeks and sixty-two weeks; it will be built again, with plaza and moat, even in times of distress. [26] "Then after the sixty-two weeks the Messiah will be cut off and have nothing, and the people of the prince who is to come will destroy the city and the sanctuary. And its end will come with a flood; even to the end there will be war; desolations are determined. [27] "And he will make a firm covenant with the many for one week, but in the middle of the week he will put a stop to sacrifice and grain offering; and on the wing of abominations will come one who makes desolate, even until a complete destruction, one that is decreed, is poured out on the one who makes desolate."

Shedding Light on Daniel 9

The 9th chapter of Daniel is one of the most profound and debated writings of the Bible. Understanding this Study Scripture is key to understanding GOD's plan of redemption and prophecy. Chapter 9 unifies the other visions in the book of Daniel, and unlocks the mysteries of their meaning. In the Study Scripture, verse 25 refers to a specific time for the coming of Messiah. The seven weeks with the sixty-two weeks combine to make 69 weeks of years (483 years) until the coming of Messiah. Most scholars agree that the starting point for the 483 years was the decree to restore and rebuild Jerusalem. This is a reference to the decree in the time of Nehemiah in the twentieth year of King Artaxerxes in 445 B.C. (Nehemiah 2:1-8). After this, Messiah would appear on the scene.

The exact point of the Messiah's appearance can be debated, but it most likely refers to the triumphal entry of Christ into Jerusalem on Palm Sunday when Jesus presented Himself and was recognized by the people as Messiah and Prince. Based on the calculations above, this event would have occurred around 30-33 A.D. and placing the time of Jesus' birth at approximately years 0-4 A.D. As mentioned in Matthew 2 -on the basis of the Micah 5:2 Study Scripture- there was a high level expectancy among studied Jewish believers hoping to meet Messiah. This explains why we see the disciples of John the Baptist, amongst many others, clearly asking Jesus if He was the "chosen one".

While Daniel and the Jewish people were in Babylonian captivity, the Angel Gabriel informed Daniel about the future of Israel and how its destiny converges with end time events that would affect the entire world. One of the key events spoken to Daniel was known as, the *Abomination of Desolation*, which was also referenced by Jesus in (Matthew 24:15). This key moment is highlighted as the half-way point in the final week of Daniel's Seventy Weeks. GOD also informs Daniel of a 3rd temple that would signify the beginning of GOD'S judgment poured out over the Earth.

I understand this foretelling of doom and gloom is sour to the taste for most. However, it is important to note this event while monitoring the unfolding of future prophetic events. At the end of this book, you will have read some of the most astounding biblical prophecies fulfilled. The forth-tellings of the Bible still persist today as we watch the world demoralize and the love of many grow cold (Matt 24:12). However, as Believers we are not shaken because we were told what to expect and we know our fate is sealed in peace and joy with GOD for eternity.

Investigative Questions

1. After reading and shedding light on Daniel 9, as well as taking the 4 previous Study Scriptures into consideration, why does the prediction of timing make the coming of Jesus more profound?

_____

_____

_____

_____

_____

2. Read Matthew 2:1. How was it that the Magi found Jesus? What is the significance of this sign? How does the object of that sign correlate with calendar events?

_____
_____
_____
_____
_____
_____
_____
_____
_____
_____
_____
_____

3. According to Matthew 2:2, who did the Magi ask for? What previous Study Scripture did they quote when speaking with the king?

_____
_____
_____
_____
_____
_____
_____

4. How does the self-declaration of Jesus in Matthew 20:28 correlate to verse 24 of the Study Scripture?

_____
_____
_____
_____
_____
_____
_____
_____
_____
_____
_____

5. How does the self-declaration of Jesus in Matthew 26:26-29 correlate to verse 24 of the Study Scripture?

Chapter 2: He Went

To Be Flogged & Crucified in Our Place

Days 8-14

Day 8
Chapter 2: Overview
He Went To Be Flogged & Crucified In Our Place

Today, when even the most minute outpatient procedures are done under anesthetics, it is difficult to embrace the brutality of the past. Typical modern people would likely be provoked to nausea at the graphic depiction of corporal punishment such as crucifixion and flogging. The sad fact is, despite our squeamishness, this ordeal was a reality for Jesus and many others. Romans were professionals at scourging and took special delight in their professionalism at punishing victims through these brutal acts.

Another prophetic scripture pointing towards the marring of Jesus is found in Isaiah 52:14, where the prophet says, *"Just as there were many who were appalled at him his appearance was so disfigured beyond that of any human being and his form marred beyond human likeness"*. Taking this scripture literally, we can conclude that during His flogging, Jesus' physical body was marred nearly beyond recognition. As appalling as this sound, it was only an overture of what was to follow. Matthew 27:26 continues to tell us, *"...and when he had scourged Jesus, he delivered him to be crucified"*. The flogging of Jesus was merely preparation for His imminent crucifixion. After graphically reminding us of the flogging endured by Jesus, Peter ecstatically reminds us in his letter found in 1 Peter 2:24, that it was by these same stripes in which we are healed. The word *healed* is the Greek word "iaomai", a word which clearly refers to physical healing, as it is a word derived from the medical term used to describe the physical healing or curing of the human body.

Usually, crucifixion was reserved for serious offenders with committed acts of treason against Rome. Jesus did not promote such acts and was innocent. With every known opportunity to escape, Jesus willfully laid down His life to fulfill the mission given to Him by GOD. Subsequent to reading Chapter 2 of this devotional study, we know His mission was to reunite GOD with HIS people forever. For many of faith, the completed mission also encompassed supernatural provision while on Earth. As you read through the Chapter, analyzing the facts, I pray you will discover what the finished mission of Jesus provided to those who believe.

Questions for the Heart

Your answers to these questions are not meant to be criticized, rather they should be analyzed. By answering honestly, this section may be used to get a gauge of where your current knowledge and heart is. Be sure to write each answer on your notepad.

1) What is your initial feeling at the thought of someone being flogged and crucified?

2) Based on your current knowledge, under what legal grounds was Jesus crucified?

3) Do you think it was fair for Jesus to be crucified? Why or why not?

4) Why would GOD allow someone HE loved to experience such agony?

5) What do you believe the flogging and crucifixion provided to Christians?

The Ten Learning Steps

The Ten Learning Steps have been provided as a guide to help you make the most of each Study Scripture. Carefully focus on each Learning Step throughout this chapter to make the most of this endeavor.

1. For those who are willing, pray to GOD- in the name of Jesus- for HIS Truth to ou.
1. Carefully read the Study Scripture at least 3 times, focusing on each minute detail.
2. Locate (online or hard copy) the Study Scripture in an amplified bible to discover the
particulars of its content.
3. On a dedicated notepad, transcribe important thoughts derived from your initial glance.
Ensure to notate portions of the Study Scripture which have the greatest relevance to you.
4. Do your best to answer the Investigative Questions section without referencing the
Study Scripture.
5. Check or complete the Investigative Questions section by using the corresponding Study Scripture.
6. Record findings, questions and additions to your dedicated your notepad.
7. Insert the location of each Study Scripture in your phone, tablet or notepad for future
reference and memorization.
8. If possible, discuss your questions and comments with spiritual leaders, mentors or
friends who can guide you through this study.
9. As led, pray for clarity regarding areas of apprehension and ask GOD for deeper understanding.

Day 9

The Psalmist Prophesies the Crucifixion of Jesus
700 Years Prior

Study Scripture: Psalms 22: 1-24 *CEB*

"My GOD! My GOD, why have you left me all alone? Why are you so far from saving me so far from my anguished groans? 2 My GOD, I cry out during the day, but you don't answer, even at nighttime I don't stop. 3 You are the holy one, enthroned.

You are Israel's praise. 4 Our ancestors trusted you they trusted you and you rescued them; 5 they cried out to you and they were saved; they trusted you and they weren't ashamed. 6 But I'm just a worm, less than human; insulted by one person, despised by another. 7 All who see me make fun of me they gape, shaking their heads: 8 "He committed himself to the Lord, so let GOD rescue him; let GOD deliver him because GOD likes him so much." 9 But you are the one who pulled me from the womb, placing me safely at my mother's breasts. 10 I was thrown on you from birth; you've been my GO since I was in my mother's womb.

11 Please don't be far from me, because trouble is near and there's no one to help. 12 Many bulls surround me; mighty bulls from Bashan encircle me. 13 They open their mouths at me like a lion ripping and roaring! 14 I'm poured out like water. All my bones have fallen apart. My heart is like wax; it melts inside me. 15 My strength is dried up like a piece of broken pottery. My tongue sticks to the roof of my mouth; you've set me down in the dirt of death. 16 Dogs surround me; a pack of evil people circle me like a lion oh, my poor hands and feet! 17 I can count all my bones! Meanwhile, they just stare at me, watching me. 18 They divvy up my garments among themselves; they cast lots for my clothes. 19 But you, Lord! Don't be far away! You are my strength! Come quick and help me! 20 Deliver me from the sword.

Deliver my life from the power of the dog. 21 Save me from the mouth of the lion. From the horns of the wild oxen you have answered me! 22 I will declare your name to my brothers and sisters; I will praise you in the very center of the congregation! 23 All of you who revere the Lord—praise him! All of you who are Jacob's descendants—honor him!

All of you who are all Israel's off spring stand in awe of him! 24 Because he didn't despise or detest the suffering of the one who suffered he didn't hide his face from me. No, he listened when I cried out to him for help."

Shedding Light on Psalms 22

There were at least 28 prophecies fulfilled on the final day of the crucifixion of Jesus Christ. Witnesses were present attesting to the perfection of each detail regarding fulfilling prophecy during the death of Jesus. Matthew, Mark, Luke, and John carefully articulated the events that mirrored the image of Psalm 22.

There are at least 12 details recorded in this psalm which match the gospel accounts, a few being Christ's pierced hands and feet (Psalms 22:16; John 20:25-28), the words spoken by those who killed Him (Psalms 22:7-8; Luke 23:35), and even Jesus' last words (Psalms 22:1; Mark 15:34). The prophecies of Christ's scourging, the tearing of His flesh, mocking, prolonged agony, and slow death were fulfilled as expressed in the Psalms.

Often, there is a concern among skeptics that Jesus could have easily fulfilled each prophecy based on His knowledge of biblical history. However, this argument is quickly defeated when met with the many historical facts which Jesus could not have controlled. For instance, the beating He received from the soldiers or their gambling (casting lots) for His garments could not have been provoked by Jesus. GOD foresaw this custom centuries before Rome existed!

Who, but GOD, could bring these events to pass 1,000 years after He inspired them to be written? Dozens of potential scriptures add prophetic details to Jesus' crucifixion, yet very few have been found as profound as this Psalms.

Investigative Questions

1. What two things did the enemies do in the psalmist's vision that was literally fulfilled at the crucifixion of Jesus (Psalm 22: 16-18)?

_____
_____
_____
_____
_____
_____
_____
_____
_____
_____

2. What 6 references does the psalmist use to describe His bodily suffering (Psalm 22: 14-15)?

_____
_____
_____
_____
_____
_____
_____
_____
_____
_____
_____

3. What scornful remark found in Psalm 22:8 was expressed at Jesus' crucifixion hundreds of years later in Matthew 27:43?

_____
_____
_____
_____

_____
_____
_____
_____
_____
_____
_____

4. How does the plea written in the Study Scripture, Psalm 22:8, correlate with Jesus' declaration during His crucifixion in Matthew 27:46?

_____
_____
_____
_____
_____
_____
_____
_____
_____
_____
_____

5. When does the psalmist suggest that Jesus began His close relationship with GOD? See Psalm 22: 9-11.

_____
_____
_____
_____
_____
_____
_____
_____
_____
_____
_____
_____

6. In your opinion, what are the possibilities that this scripture could have predicted the events of the crucifixion of Jesus? Why?

_____

_____

_____

_____

_____

_____

_____

_____

_____

_____

_____

Study Scripture: Matthew 27:15-26

"15 At the (Passover) festival the governor's custom was to release to the crowd a prisoner they wanted. 16 At that time they had a notorious prisoner called Barabbas. 17 So when they had gathered together, Pilate said to them, "Who is it you want me to release for you—Barabbas, or Jesus who is called Messiah?" 18 For he knew they had handed Him over because of envy. 19 While he was sitting on the judge's bench, his wife sent word to him, "Have nothing to do with that righteous man, for today I've suffered terribly in a dream because of Him!" 20 The chief priests and the elders, however, persuaded the crowds to ask for Barabbas and to execute Jesus. 21 The governor asked them, "Which of the two do you want me to release for you?" "Barabbas!" they answered. 22 Pilate asked them, "What should I do then with Jesus, who is called Messiah? "They all answered, "Crucify Him!" 23 Then he said, "Why? What has He done wrong?"But they kept shouting, "Crucify Him!" all the more. 24 When Pilate saw that he was getting nowhere, but that a riot was starting instead, he took some water, washed his hands in front of the crowd, and said, "I am innocent of this man's blood. See to it yourselves!" 25 All the people answered, "His blood be on us and on our children!" 26 Then he released Barabbas to them. But after having Jesus flogged, he handed Him over to be crucified."

Shedding Light on Matthew 27

Often times, malevolent men do not meet the consequences of the crimes they commit. Even worse, innocent men are often recipients of the punishments designed for criminals. Jesus' execution is a conspiracy of empowered abuse and abandonment of honorable duty. The Jewish high priest, Caiaphas, and his co-conspirators predetermined the outcome of the trial of Jesus and needed the foundation of evidence. They arranged for false testimony, but still could not condemn the innocent Jesus. Consequently, it takes Caiaphas's direct involvement to incite charges of blasphemy. Since the position of high priest cannot legally order someone to death, Caiaphas turns to Pilate to fulfill his purpose.

When the high priest brought Jesus to the Roman courts, Pilate expressed he had no malice against Jesus and labored to discharge him. Pilate was persuaded even further when he received an alarming warning from his wife. Despite opposing confessions, the hearts of the Jewish leaders remained hardened and their assault on Jesus advanced. Pilate attempts to defuse an increasingly rabid crowd by offering Jesus to be flogged and pardoned in exchange for the execution of a known criminal named Barabbas. When asked to choose between the two men, the irate crowd responded with a strong decision. Eventually, Pilate defers to their passions rather than justice.

Most readers are instinctively upset when they read the circumstances regarding the false conviction of Jesus. However, let us look at this story from another perspective. What if you were set free for a crime you committed? Unlike Barabbas, assume you were remorseful about your illicit actions. Assume that you had no say because your release was a demand. Surely, you would have compassion for the stranger who took your place. The questions is, *what would you have done with your new found freedom*? Would you take on a new perspective of life or would you revert to the same behaviors which caused your affliction? Believe it or not, as we will soon see, these questions are still pertinent today.

Investigative Questions

1. During which Jewish Festival was Jesus handed over to Pilate? In your opinion, what is the significance of Jesus being handed over in such a sacrificial manner during this time? *See Matt. 27:15.*

_____

_____

_____

_____

_____

_____

_____

_____

_____

_____

2. What did GOD reveal to Pilate's wife in a dream (Matt. 27:19)?

_____

_____

_____

_____

_____

_____

_____

_____

_____

2. Pilate referred to Barabbas as a notorious prisoner and suggested Jesus had committed no legitimate crime. When asked, who did the crowd choose to punish? *See Matt. 27:21.*

_____

_____

_____

_____

_____

_____

_____

_____

_____

_____

_____

4. What punishment did the crowd elect for Jesus (*See Matt. 27:22*)?

_____

_____

_____

_____

_____

_____

_____

_____

_____

_____

5. What was Pilate's response to the crowd's demands to punish Jesus (Matt. *27: 24*)?

_____

_____

_____

_____

_____

_____

_____

_____

_____

_____

_____

_____

6. Do you find it fair that Barabbas was released and Jesus was not? How does this situation mirror the relationship between Christ and mankind?

_____

_____

_____

_____

_____

_____

_____

_____

Study Scripture: John 19:1-11

"¹Then Pilate took Jesus and flogged him. ² And the soldiers twisted together a crown of thorns and put it on his head and arrayed him in a purple robe. ³They came up to him, saying, "Hail, King of the Jews!" and struck him with their hands. 4 Pilate went out again and said to them, "See, I am bringing him out to you that you may know that I find no guilt in him." 5 So Jesus came out, wearing the crown of thorns and the purple robe. Pilate said to them, "Behold the man!" 6 When the chief priests and the officers saw him, they cried out, "Crucify him, crucify him!" Pilate said to them, "Take him yourselves and crucify him, for I find no guilt in him." 7 The Jews answered him, "We have a law, and according to that law he ought to die because he has made himself the Son of GOD." 8 When Pilate heard this statement, he was even more afraid. 9 He entered his headquarters again and said to Jesus, "Where are you from?" But Jesus gave him no answer. 10 So Pilate said to him, "You will not speak to me? Do you not know that I have authority to release you and authority to crucify you?"11 Jesus answered him, "You would have no authority over me at all unless it had been given you from above. Therefore he who delivered me over to you has the greater sin."

Shedding Light on John 19

There is often much confusion among new Believers regarding the difference between John the Baptist and John the Apostle. For clarity, John the Baptist was the cousin of Jesus who performed his water baptism. John was later beheaded during the beginning of the Jesus' ministry. John the disciple, later turned Apostle, was one of Jesus' inner circle members and the writer of several books in the New Testament. One of the most fascinating aspects of John's writings regarding the matter of the flogging of Jesus, was that he was an eye witness. When the other disciples fled at Jesus' capture, John remained to tell the story of the flogging of Jesus.

Scourging, called *verberatio* by the Romans, was the worst flogging administered by the courts. While the Jews oversaw corporal punishment in the synagogues for certain offenses, these were minor compared to scourging. Scourging was not a formal form of execution, but it was brutal enough to be fatal in many cases. It's purpose was not only to cause excruciating pain, but to encourage humiliation.

Consistent with everything surrounding His death, Jesus knew He would be scourged (Matt. 20:19). Jesus explained to His disciples that before He died from the torture of the cross He must endure a brutal beating at the hands of the Romans. In Luke 22, moments before His capture, we are told Jesus deeply agonized over His fate He asked GOD to take away His pending punishment if it were at all possible. Jesus responded to the inaudible response by exclaiming, not my will but your will be done. He embraced vicious scourging as His body was ripped open at the whipping post. Surely, there must have been a strong conviction and purpose for Him to remain steady on His path.

I would like to re-emphasize that even Jesus, filled with the power of the Holy Spirit, had human moments of despair, doubt, and unbelief. I believe the writers of the gospel inserted this key bit of information without imagining the impact it would have thousands of years later. If you serve or are considering serving GOD, you can take refuge in knowing HE understands the pain and inequities of this world. More importantly, HE understands that you will have moments when you will not project courage and grace. Again, HE understands and HE will still be there with open arms to embrace you.

Investigative Questions

1. Pilate sought only to flog and release Jesus. Jesus was ultimately flogged and crucified. What is the prophetic significance of Jesus being flogged and crucified (John 19:26 and Isaiah 53)?

_____
_____
_____
_____
_____
_____
_____
_____
_____
_____

2. What was Pilate's purpose for humiliating Jesus before the Jewish leaders if he believed in His innocence (John 19:4)?

_____

_____

_____

_____

_____

_____

_____

_____

_____

3. What reason did the Jewish Leaders give for demanding Jesus be crucified and killed? Was there anything Jesus could have done to prevent this, if so what (John 19: 7)?

_____

_____

_____

_____

_____

_____

4. According to Jesus, who gave Pilate authority to crucify Him (See John 19:11 and John 3:16)?

_____

_____

_____

_____

_____

_____

_____

_____

5. It seems as though Jesus had ample opportunities to prevent imminent harm to Himself. Why did Jesus provide Pilate with a response that would have caused Himself to receive punishment?

_____

_____

_____

_____

_____

_____

_____

_____

6. What correlations do you see between the events in the Study Scripture and the prophecies of Isaiah 53?

_____

_____

_____

_____

_____

_____

_____

_____

_____

_____

_____

_____

Day 12
Jesus Crucified

Study Scripture: Matthew 27:32-44

"32 As they went out, they found a man of Cyrene, Simon by name. They compelled this man to carry his cross. 33 And when they came to a place called Golgotha (which means Place of a Skull), 34 they offered him wine to drink, mixed with gall, but when he tasted it, he would not drink it.35 And when they had crucified him, they divided his garments among them by casting lots. 36 Then they sat down and kept watch over him there. 37 And over his head they put the charge against him, which read, "This is Jesus, the King of the Jews." 38 Then two robbers were crucified with him, one on the right and one on the left. 39 And those who passed by derided him, wagging their heads 40 and saying, "You who would destroy the temple and rebuild it in three days, save yourself! If you are the Son of GOD, come down from the cross." 41 So also the chief priests, with the scribes and elders, mocked him, saying, 42 "He saved others; he cannot save himself. He is the King of Israel; let him come down now from the cross, and we will believe in him. 43 He trusts in GOD; let GOD deliver him now, if he desires him. For he said, 'I am the Son of GOD.'" 44 And the robbers who were crucified with him also reviled him in the same way.45 Now from the sixth hour there was darkness over all the land until the ninth hour. 46 And about the ninth hour Jesus cried out with a loud voice, saying, "Eli, Eli, lema sabachthani?" that is, "My GOD, my GOD, why have you forsaken me?" 47 And some of the bystanders, hearing it, said, "This man is calling Elijah." 48 And one of them at once ran and took a sponge, filled it with sour wine, and put it on a reed and gave it to him to drink."

Shedding Light on Matthew 27

Am I prepared to die? This question often provokes introspection, particularly as we advance in age. Let's face it, none of us can avoid the inevitable. We can try to avoid it, but the reality is we will all leave this material world at some point. Death often involves mental and physical suffering for those affected. Fortunately, for Believers, love is stronger than death. John states it best, *"For God so loved the world that he gave us his only Son, that whoever believes in him should not perish but have eternal life"* (John 3:16).

Jesus embraced the cross knowing it was the Father's will and the Father's way for him to die. Consistent with a criminal condemned to death by Roman law, He was forced to carry His own cross to the distant execution site established for Him. This prolonged walk of shame inflicted weight that bowed the head and back into a posture of submission. Jesus collapsed under the weight of His cross and could go no further. The Roman soldiers compelled a man named Simon to carry it for him. Simon traveled a long distance from Cyrene (in North Africa, present-day Libya) to Jerusalem for the Passover feast. One could assume the last thing he wanted to do was participate in the public execution of a criminal. Ultimately, He had little choice since Roman authority could not be challenged without serious consequences. Here is Jesus beaten, humiliated, exhausted, and reliant on a stranger to help him -even in his innocence.

Historically, the Romans were the only group who utilized the vicious practice of execution by crucifixion. Once at the execution site, a cross was laid on the ground, the hands and feet of Jesus were viciously nailed to it, the cross was then lifted up and fixed upright so the weight of His body hung on the nails. The brutality of this death was no surprise for Him. As you read through the four gospels of Matthew, Mark, Luke and John, you will find multiple times where Jesus mentions His predestined fate. Would He have allowed Himself to be hung if He did not believe in His purpose? The questions on the next page will guide you in a direction which will help you answer this inquiry.

Investigative Questions

1. Verse 35 of the Study Scripture states the soldiers divided the garments of Jesus and casted lots, or gambled for them. What verse in Psalms 22 foretells this account?

_____
_____
_____
_____
_____
_____
_____
_____
_____
_____
_____

2. Verse 38 of the Study Scripture stated Jesus was crucified between two criminals. What verse in Psalms 22 foretells this account?

_____
_____
_____
_____
_____
_____
_____
_____
_____

3. Matthew 27:41 stated that Jesus' enemies taunted Him by saying, "*He trusts in God, let God deliver Him if He wants Him*". What verse in Psalms 22 foretells this account?

_____
_____
_____
_____
_____
_____

4. David, the known author of Psalms 22 died in his old age and was not crucified. In your opinion, why would he have written such a graphic passage?

_____
_____
_____
_____
_____
_____
_____
_____
_____

_____

_____

_____

5. There were many eye witnesses who dictated the account of the crucifixion. They wrote what they saw so you would know that Jesus fulfilled prophecy. Based on what you've learned so far, what are your thoughts on the crucifixion of Jesus?

_____

_____

_____

_____

_____

_____

_____

_____

_____

_____

_____

_____

_____

_____

_____

_____

_____

_____

Study Scripture Matthew 27:50-56

"50 And Jesus cried out again with a loud voice and yielded up his spirit 51 and behold, the curtain of the temple was torn in two, from top to bottom. And the earth shook, and the rocks were split. 52 The tombs also were opened. And many bodies of the saints who had fallen asleep were raised, 53 and coming out of the tombs after his resurrection they went into the holy city and appeared to many.54 When the centurion and those who were with him, keeping watch over Jesus, saw the earthquake and what took place, they were filled with awe and said, "Truly this was the Son of God!"55 There were also many women there, looking on from a distance, who had followed Jesus from Galilee, ministering to him, 56 among whom were Mary Magdalene and Mary the mother of James and Joseph and the mother of the sons of Zebedee."

Shedding Light on Matthew 27

"Surrender!" What does this word tell you? In literal terms, surrender means to relinquish something to someone. It could also mean to yield over something granted to you such as possessions, authority, or desires. Christian leaders often minister about living a surrendered life for God. But what does it mean, exactly? The surrendered life is the act of giving back to God the life He granted you. It's relinquishing control, rights, power, direction, as well as all the things you say and do. It's totally resigning your life over to His hands, to do with you as He pleases. At first, this idea may cause you to be petrified. Nevertheless, the closer you come to understanding the Heart of God, the more you will be assured that His plans for you are greater than you could have ever imagined.

Jesus himself lived a surrendered life. He did nothing on His own. He made no move and spoke no word without being instructed by the Father.

A few examples of His outlook on sacrifice include:

1) *"I came down from heaven, not to do mine own will, but the will of him that sent me"* (John 6:38).

2) *"I seek not mine own glory"* (John 8:50).

3) *"I do nothing of myself; but as my Father hath taught me, I speak these things...for I do always those things that please him"* (John 8:28-29).

Jesus' full surrender to God set the bar for how we ought to live. Some may insinuate Jesus had a supernatural inclination to follow God much more than the average person. However, the surrendered life is not imposed upon anyone—including Jesus. In Luke 22:42, Jesus clarifies that He did not want to die in such a horrible fashion, but would do what God had instructed. The death of Jesus reflected in the Study Scripture depicts the power of His sacrifice. Through the chain of supernatural occurrences, witness were convicted that His surrendered life was honored by God.

Investigative Questions

1. Who caused Jesus to die after He was on the cross (Matt.27: 50)?

_____
_____
_____
_____
_____
_____
_____
_____
_____
_____
_____

2. Read *John 10:17-18*. Where did Jesus get His authority over life and death?

_____

_____

_____

_____

_____

_____

_____

_____

_____

3. Verse 51 of the Study Scripture says the veil of the Jewish Temple was torn when Jesus died. The writers of the New Testament were Jewish and part of the community. If they devised the tearing of the temple veil, would this passage have survived for thousands of years? Why or Why not?

_____

_____

_____

_____

_____

_____

_____

_____

_____

4. Verse 52-53 of the Study Scripture says the dead rose and began to walk around the city after the death of Jesus. Considering the relatively small community of Jerusalem at that time, would this passage have survived for thousands of years? Why or Why not?

_____

_____

_____

_____

_____

_____

_____
_____
_____

5. Verse 54 of the Study Scripture says after the death of Jesus the earth shook and the Roman centurion began to believe that Jesus was the Son of God. Who was there to witness this event? Why would the writers concoct such an unbelievable story if they wanted people to believe?

_____
_____
_____
_____
_____
_____
_____
_____
_____

6. The events in this Study Scripture may be hard to digest. Would it have been more appropriate if these events were left out? In your opinion, why did the disciples insert these moments into their writings?

_____
_____
_____
_____
_____
_____
_____
_____
_____
_____
_____
_____

Study Scripture: John 19:31-37

"31 Since it was the day of Preparation, and so that the bodies would not remain on the cross on the Sabbath (for that Sabbath was a high day), the Jews asked Pilate that their legs might be broken and that they might be taken away. 32 So the soldiers came and broke the legs of the first, and of the other who had been crucified with him. 33 But when they came to Jesus and saw that he was already dead, they did not break his legs. 34 But one of the soldiers pierced his side with a spear, and at once there came out blood and water. 35 He who saw it has borne witness—his testimony is true, and he knows that he is telling the truth—that you also may believe. 36 For these things took place that the Scripture might be fulfilled: "Not one of his bones will be broken." 37 And again another Scripture says, "They will look on him whom they have pierced."

Shedding Light on John 19

The Jewish leaders showed more mercy than their Roman counterparts regarding the treatment of criminals. It was Roman practice to leave a crucified man on the cross until he died. It was not unusual for someone to hang for days on the cross before they expired. Once deceased, the body was not given a burial. Instead, it was left to be exposed for the vultures and dogs to feed upon.

However, The Law of Moses treated crucifixion differently by stating, *"And if a man has committed a crime punishable by death and he is put to death, and you hang him on a tree, his body shall not remain all night upon the tree, but you shall bury him the same day" (Deut.21:22-23).* On this occasion it was even more important that the bodies be buried before evening since the Sabbath was about to begin.

John 19 reflects happenings which are hard to imagine. The breaking of legs and a conspiracy to ensure murder are only two circumstances it depicts. One incident often noted is the piercing of the side or possibly the heart of Jesus. In true prophetic fashion, Jesus eluded to the very idea of the piercing of His heart with an outpouring of water. In John 7:38 Jesus said, *"He who believes in me, as the scripture has said, 'Out of his heart shall flow rivers of living water".* Jesus knew His execution would empower lives and provide salvation for many. This statement is not meant to suggest the physical execution of His Believers. Instead, Jesus establishes that like Him, those who believe and will sacrifice can provide life to the sick and broken hearted through their relative sacrifices. What a wonderful analogy!

Investigative Questions

1. According to verse 31 of the Study Scripture, on what holiday was Jesus executed? Read Exodus 12 and explain the parallels between the two events.

_____
_____
_____
_____
_____
_____
_____
_____
_____
_____
_____
_____
_____
_____

2. What did the Jewish leaders request to be done to Jesus in verse 31 of the Study Scripture? What would this have caused if Jesus was still alive? *Additional research may be required to answer this question.*

_____
_____
_____

_____

_____

_____

_____

_____

_____

_____

_____

3. Did the Roman centurion break the legs of the two criminals? Did the centurion break the legs of Jesus? How does this account correlate with Exodus 12:46 and Psalm 34:20?

_____

_____

_____

_____

_____

_____

_____

_____

_____

_____

_____

_____

4. Why did the Roman centurion pierce the side of Jesus? Why did water and blood flow from His body? How does this account correlate with Zachariah 12:10, Isaiah 53:5, and Psalm 22:14?

_____

_____

_____

_____

_____

_____

_____

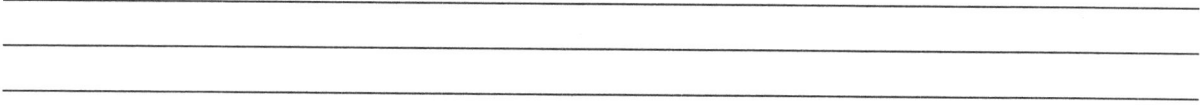

Chapter 3: He Came
Back from the Dead and Rose His Physical Body
Days 15-20

Day 15
Chapter 3: Overview
He Came, Back From The Dead and Rose
His Physical Body

The most important fact I hope to convey through this chapter is that Jesus resurrected His physical body. Any religion or intellectual text which subscribes to a spiritual, ghostly resurrection has missed the cornerstone of the Christian faith. Had Jesus resurrected only in spiritual form He would not have a legitimate claim to defeating death. The bodily resurrection of Jesus Christ from the dead is the crowning proof of Christianity. Everything else said or done by Christ and the Apostles is secondary in importance to the resurrection. If the resurrection did not take place, then Christianity is a false religion. If it took place, then Jesus Christ is God and the Christian faith is absolute truth.

Jesus understood that although His disciples witnessed great miracles in His midst, they still had not come to a full understanding of how He would fulfill prophecy. In Matthew 17:22, Jesus tells His disciples of His pending betrayal, execution, and raising from the dead on the third day. Despite Jesus making His pre-ordained sacrifice abundantly clear to his disciples, they were still shocked at both His crucifixion and resurrection.

The Resurrection proves the unmatchable divinity of Jesus Christ. The fact Jesus Christ died on the cross does not prove He is God. Jesus proved His deity by fulfilling the prophecies of His death and by His return from the grave—which is the best part!
It is the physical resurrection of Christ is the Believers' pathway to eternal life.

Questions for the Heart

Your answers to these questions are not meant to be criticized; rather, they should be analyzed. Use this section to get a gauge of where your current knowledge and heart are by answering honestly. Be sure to write each answer on your notepad.

1) What is your initial thought when you consider the reality of Jesus raising from death after His brutal scourging?

2) In your opinion, is there any possibility Jesus did not actually die on the cross? Why or why not?

3) In your opinion, is it at all possible that the disciples of Jesus could have staged His death? Why or why not?

4) Based on your current knowledge, who assigned the guards at the tomb of Jesus and why?

5) Do you believe Christianity would have continued if Jesus had not risen from the dead? Why or why not?

The Ten Learning Steps

The Ten Learning Steps have been provided as a guide to help you make the most of each Study Scripture. Carefully focus on each Learning Step throughout this chapter to make the most of this endeavor.

1. For those who are willing, pray to GOD— in the name of Jesus— for HIS Truth to be revealed to you.
2. Carefully read the Study Scripture at least 3 times, focusing on each minute detail.
3. Locate (online or hard copy) the Study Scripture in an *Amplified* Bible to discover the particulars of its content.
4. On a dedicated notepad, write important thoughts derived from your initial glance.
   Ensure to notate portions of the Study Scripture which have the greatest relevance to you.
5. Do your best to answer the Investigative Questions section without referencing the Study Scripture.
6. Check or complete the Investigative Questions section by using the corresponding Study Scripture.
7. Record findings, questions and additions to your dedicated notepad.
8. Insert the location of each Study Scripture in your phone, tablet or notepad for future reference and memorization.
9. If possible, discuss your questions and comments with spiritual leaders, mentors, or friends who can guide you through this study.
10. As led, pray for clarity regarding areas of apprehension and ask GOD for deeper understanding.

Day 16
Jesus Foretells His Death and Ressurection

Study Scripture: Matthew 20:17-19

"17And Jesus going up to Jerusalem took the twelve disciples apart ° in the way, and said unto them, 18 Behold, we go up to Jerusalem; and the Son of man shall be betrayed unto the chief priests and unto the scribes, and they shall condemn him to death, 19 And shall deliver him to the Gentiles to mock, and to scourge, and to crucify him: and the third day he shall rise again."

Shedding Light on Matthew 20

In this chapter Matthew, one of the disciples, informs us of Jesus' prediction of His own crucifixion and resurrection. The very fact that Jesus foresaw His imminent fate speaks to His profound relationship with God. Of the world's foremost religions, there are no known spiritual leaders who make the claim they would awaken from their death except for Jesus.

The first time we find Jesus speaking about being raised from the dead was during the beginning of his ministry. When asked for a sign, He gave them the sign of the temple, which was figurative for his body. On another occasion, when asked for a sign, He gave them the sign of Jonah. As Jonah was three days in the belly of the sea creature so Jesus will be three days in the earth. He also privately told His disciples the details about his death and resurrection.

Jesus was also known for making public statements about His resurrection. This claim incited the religious leaders to request a guard at His tomb. There would be no need for a guard unless He had predicted His resurrection from the dead.

Investigative Questions

1. Who did Jesus foretell His future to? Based on your current knowledge, did they believe or understand what Jesus was saying *(Matt. 20:17)*?

_____

_____

_____

_____

_____

_____

_____

_____

_____

_____

2. Where did Jesus say He would be betrayed? Based on what you read in Chapter 3 was He correct *(Matt 20:18)*?

_____

_____

_____

_____

_____

_____

_____

_____

_____

_____

3. Who did Jesus say would condemn Him to death? Based on what you've read in Chapter 3, was He correct *(v.18)*?

_____

_____

_____

_____

_____

_____

_____
_____
_____
_____
_____

4. Who did Jesus say would mock, scourge, and crucify Him *(v. 19)*?

_____
_____
_____
_____
_____
_____
_____
_____
_____

5. In your opinion, explain the chances of Jesus guessing the place, the people, and the chain of events regarding His execution? Explain what was and was not within His control.

_____
_____
_____
_____
_____
_____
_____
_____
_____

Study Scripture: John 19:38-42

"38 After these things Joseph of Arimathea, who was a disciple of Jesus, but secretly for fear of the Jews, asked Pilate that he might take away the body of Jesus, and Pilate gave him permission. So he came and took away his body. 39 Nicodemus also, who earlier had come to Jesus by night, came bringing a mixture of myrrh and aloes, about seventy-five pounds in weight. 40 So they took the body of Jesus and bound it in linen cloths with the spices, as is the burial custom of the Jews. 41 Now in the place where he was crucified there was a garden, and in the garden a new tomb in which no one had yet been laid. 42 So because of the Jewish day of Preparation, since the tomb was close at hand, they laid Jesus there."

<u>Shedding Light on John 19</u>

Please allow me to shed light on the Study Scripture by highlighting four points:

Point #1: After His crucifixion, Jesus was buried in a tomb by Joseph of Arimathea. This is a highly significant fact. Contrary to critics like John Dominic Crossan of the Jesus Seminar, the location of Jesus' burial site was known to Jew and Christian alike. In such case, the disciples could never have proclaimed His resurrection in Jerusalem if the tomb had not been empty.

Point #2: As a member of the Jewish court who condemned Jesus, Joseph of Arimathea is unlikely to be a Christian invention. There was strong resentment against the Jewish leadership for their role in the condemnation of Jesus (I Thess. 2.15). It is therefore highly improbable Christians could interject the story of a member of the Jewish court honoring Jesus by giving him a proper burial. It would be more probable that Joseph would have allowed Jesus to be dispatched as a common criminal.

Point #3: No other competing burial story exists. If the burial by Joseph were fictitious, then we would expect to find either some historical trace of what happened to Jesus' corpse, or at least some category of competing legends. Instead, all known sources are unanimous on Jesus' honorable committal by Joseph.

Point #4: The earliest Jewish allegation of the disciples stealing Jesus' body in Matthew 28:15, shows the body was missing from the tomb. The earliest Jewish response to the disciples' proclamation, *"He is risen from the dead!"*, was not to point to His occupied tomb and to laugh them off as fanatics. Instead, it was to claim that they had taken away Jesus' body. Therefore, we have evidence of the empty tomb from the very opponents of the early Christians.

Investigative Questions

1. Whose tomb was Jesus buried in? Did Jesus request to be buried there? How was the burial was arranged *(vs. 38)*?

_____

_____

_____

_____

_____

_____

_____

_____

_____

_____

2. Read Isaiah 53:9 and explain correlations between the scripture and question 1. Was the book of Isaiah written before Jesus' burial?

_____

_____

_____

_____

_____

_____

_____

_____

_____

_____

_____

3. Roman soldiers were trained executers. In your opinion, would Pilate have given Joseph the body of Jesus if he doubted He was truly dead?

_____

_____

_____

_____

_____

_____

_____

_____

_____

_____

_____

_____

4. How many pounds of myrrh and aloe was Jesus buried and bound with? Would it have been possible for Jesus to breathe if He was still alive (vs.39)?

_____

_____

_____

_____

_____

_____

_____

_____

_____

_____

5. Joseph and Nicodemus were members of the Jewish Temple which convicted and sentenced Jesus. In your opinion, why would they be concerned with the burial of Jesus?

_____

_____

_____

_____

_____

_____

_____

_____

_____

_____

_____

6. In your opinion, based on the factual basis of Jesus' crucifixion, do you believe there were any opportunities for Jesus to have been buried while alive? Why or why not?

_____

_____

_____

_____

_____

_____

_____

_____

_____

_____

_____

Day 18
Trained Guards at the Tomb of Jesus

Study Scripture: Matthew 27:62-65

"⁶²The next day, that is, after the day of Preparation, the chief priests and the Pharisees gathered before Pilate ⁶³ and said, "Sir, we remember how that impostor said, while he was still alive, 'After three days I will rise.' ⁶⁴ Therefore order the tomb to be made secure until the third day, lest his disciples go and steal him away and tell the people, 'He has risen from the dead,' and the last fraud will be worse than the first." ⁶⁵ Pilate said to them, "You have a guard of soldiers. Go, make it as secure as you can." ⁶⁶ So they went and made the tomb secure by sealing the stone and setting a guard."

Shedding Light on Matthew 27

Since the battalion mentioned in the Study Scripture were Roman guards, then four is the minimum that protocol would allow for a regiment of this nature. Earlier in the account of Jesus' punishment we were offered a glimpse of this basic squad unit. In John we read that the soldiers divided his garments *"into four parts, one part for each soldier"* (John 19:23). At the conservative bare minimum, we must say there were at least four.

If we look at the matter from the basis of the evidence rather than from art work and conventional presentation, it becomes clear there were likely much over four. Let's begin with Matthew 27:64. It is here that Pharisees approached Pilate for guards because, *"Otherwise, His disciples may come and steal the body and tell the people that He has been raised from the dead. This last deception will be worse than the first."* Pilate responds by saying, *"Take a Guard"*.

Although there is ambiguity here in the Greek, I believe the context affirms that a mentionable amount of Roman soldiers were dispatched. By *a guard* it would be like saying a "squad", where the singular implies a plurality. If Pilate had said, *"Take a Legion"*, we wouldn't foolishly believe he appointed just one man.

Pilate then tells them to make the tomb *as secure as they know how*. Imagine exactly how many guards they would have sent if they feared Jesus' disciples stealing the body. Well, at the minimum, you know there are 11 disciples. In that case, I imagine if you are trying to thwart them, it would be supposed that one would have at least one soldier per known potential human threat. Having served in two military conflicts, I pay close notice to military strategy. Personally, I would have sent at least 20 Roman guards as a conservative, but safe estimate. Remember that days earlier, large crowds throughout Jerusalem were shouting and singing *"Hosanna"* or *"Savior"*, as Jesus entered the city. In other words, the Romans and chief priests knew Jesus had not only 11 disciples, but 11,000 or more (He miraculously fed over 5,000 men during His ministry). How many guards would you have sent? Well, I think you caught my point.

Investigative Questions

1. What did the Pharisees explain to Pilate regarding the resurrection of Jesus *(v. 63)*?

_____

_____

_____

_____

_____

_____

_____

_____

_____

_____

_____

_____

2. What did the Pharisees do to ensure the tomb was not opened on the third day?

_____

_____

_____

_____

_____

_____

_____

_____

_____

_____

_____

3. Matthew 28:11-15 says the Pharisees paid the Roman guards to say the body of Jesus was stolen by the disciples. Would you consider this the Pharisees acknowledgment of an empty tomb? Why or why not?

_____

_____

_____

_____

_____

_____

_____

_____

_____

4. In your opinion, if the disciples secretly retrieved the body of Jesus, why would they be willing to go to death to continue His works? What was their motive?

_____

_____

_____

_____

_____

_____

_____

_____

_____

_____

_____

_____

_____

_____

5. Would you go to death by capital punishment to defend the lies of another individual? Why or why not?

_____

_____

_____

_____

_____

_____

_____

_____

_____

_____

_____

_____

_____

_____

_____

_____

_____

_____

_____

_____

_____

_____

Study Scripture: Luke 24:1-12

"1 But on the first day of the week, at early dawn, they went to the tomb, taking the spices they had prepared. 2 And they found the stone rolled away from the tomb,3 but when they went in they did not find the body of the Lord Jesus. 4While they were perplexed about this, behold, two men stood by them in dazzling apparel. 5And as they were frightened and bowed their faces to the ground, the men said to them, "Why do you seek the living among the dead? 6 He is not here, but has risen. Remember how he told you, while he was still in Galilee, 7 that the Son of Man must be delivered into the hands of sinful men and be crucified and on the third day rise."8 And they remembered his words, 9 and returning from the tomb they told all these things to the eleven and to all the rest. 10 Now it was Mary Magdalene and Joanna and Mary the mother of James and the other women with them who told these things to the apostles, 11 but these words seemed to them an idle tale, and they did not believe them. 12 But Peter rose and ran to the tomb; stooping and looking in, he saw the linen cloths by themselves; and he went home marveling at what had happened."

<u>Shedding Light on Luke 24</u>

Where were the remaining 11 disciples of Jesus on the day of His resurrection? Rather than proclaiming a message of a victorious and risen Savior, we find the disciples in retreat, disappointed, and perplexed. Glittered with sadness and confusion they were seeking their next steps. But didn't Jesus pre-warn His disciples of what would happen? The answer is yes.

It should encourage you to know that Jesus' own disciples frequently didn't understand what He was teaching or doing. The scriptures repeatedly tell us that although they had a perfect Teacher, they often failed to understand Him correctly. Nevertheless, Jesus used them. This demonstrated the disciples' success resulted from God's work, not human achievement. It's also interesting to notice in the scripture that Jesus appeared first to Mary Magdalene, out of whom He had driven seven demons.

She was chosen as the first person to see the risen Christ. However, when Mary Magdalene went to convey to Jesus' disciples she had seen Jesus risen from the dead, they didn't believe her. Was it because when considering her past, they viewed her as being mentally and emotionally unstable? Was it her gender? Was it their complete lack of belief?

What matters most is that despite– and possibly because of her past– Jesus trusted Mary Magdalene with the most important news that mankind has ever known. I believe this act clearly shows the heart of Jesus–trusting, guiding, and willing to use those that have been overlooked and underestimated by others.

Investigative Questions

1. Which day of the week was Jesus Risen *(v. 1)*?

_____
_____
_____
_____
_____
_____
_____
_____
_____
_____

2. If Jesus was in the tomb for three days and three nights when was He crucified, how does this contradict the current holiday known as Easter?
   Self-study of the Feast of Passover is recommended to better understand the correlation of the crucifixion of Jesus.

_____
_____
_____
_____
_____
_____
_____
_____
_____
_____

3. What did the two men at the tomb remind Mary about *(v. 6-8)*?

_____
_____
_____
_____
_____
_____
_____

3. When expressed by Mary, did the disciples believe Jesus was risen from the dead *(v. 11)*?

_____
_____
_____
_____
_____
_____
_____

5. How does the perceived faithlessness of the disciples impact your faith, whether positively or negatively?

_____
_____
_____
_____
_____
_____
_____
_____
_____
_____

Study Scripture Luke 24:36-49

"36 As they were talking about these things, Jesus himself stood among them, and said to them, "Peace to you!" 37 But they were startled and frightened and thought they saw a spirit. 38 And he said to them, "Why are you troubled, and why do doubts arise in your hearts? 39 See my hands and my feet, that it is I myself. Touch me, and see. For a spirit does not have flesh and bones as you see that I have." 40 And when he had said this, he showed them his hands and his feet. 41 And while they still disbelieved for joy and were marveling, he said to them, "Have you anything here to eat?" 42 They gave him a piece of broiled fish, 43 and he took it and ate before them.

44 Then he said to them, "These are my words that I spoke to you while I was still with you, that everything written about me in the Law of Moses and the Prophets and the Psalms must be fulfilled." 45 Then he opened their minds to understand the Scriptures, 46 and said to them, "Thus it is written, that the Christ should suffer and on the third day rise from the dead, 47 and that repentance and forgiveness of sins should be proclaimed in his name to all nations, beginning from Jerusalem. 48 You are witnesses of these things."

Shedding Light on Luke 24

Now, of course, skeptics have tried to avoid the testimony of these numerous post-resurrection appearances of Christ by pointing out various proposed contradictions in the six accounts which list them (Matthew 28:8-20; Mark 16:9-20; Luke 24:13-51; John 20:11-21, 14; Acts 1:1-11; 1 Corinthians 15:5-8). Others charge the writers with fabricating the stories themselves. There is not a shortage of criticism regarding the resurrection of Jesus. As stated initially in this book, I embrace constructive criticism as a platform for productive dialogue. Yet, please notice my continued emphasis on the word *"constructive"*.

The mere fact that there appears to be several superficial discrepancies in the account is clear proof the writers were not engaged in some collusion. If they were in the practice of making up the story, each evidently was doing so independently of all others. This would be quite a remarkable state of affairs, especially since these discrepancies all vanish when compared under close examination. A well-known rule of evidence evaluation suggests testimonies of several witnesses, each reporting from his own particular vantage point, provide the strongest possible evidence on matters of fact. When the testimonies contain superficial contradictions, often they are resolved upon close and careful examination. This is certainly the case for the resurrection of Jesus.

I invite you to analyze the verses above in great detail. Start by analyzing the subtle differences and then begin the process of self-study. There is more Christian apologetics-based information available to educate and support you in reconciling the differences.

Investigative Questions

1. What were the disciples' reactions when Jesus appeared to them *(v. 37-39)*?

_____

_____

_____

_____

_____

_____

_____

_____

_____

_____

_____

2. What does Jesus affirm to His disciples about the reality of His resurrection *(v. 39-40)*?

_____

_____

_____

_____

_____

_____

_____

_____
_____

3. In your opinion, what was the purpose of Jesus expressing His hunger and then eating with the disciples?

_____
_____
_____
_____
_____
_____
_____
_____
_____
_____

4. Who does Jesus say the prophecies within Law of Moses, Prophets, and Psalms (also known as the Jewish Tanach or Christian Old Testament) were written about (v. 45)?

_____
_____
_____
_____
_____
_____
_____
_____
_____
_____
_____

4. What did Jesus say His crucifixion and resurrection provided for "*All Nations*" (*vv. 46-47*)?

_____
_____
_____
_____
_____
_____
_____
_____
_____
_____

6. Who were the witnesses to the events mentioned in the Study Scripture (*v. 48*)?

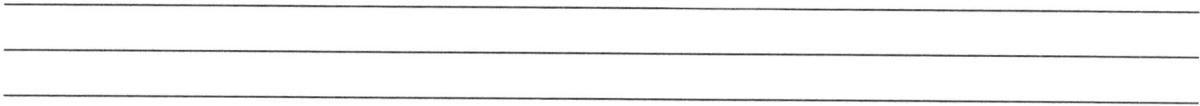

Chapter 4: He Went
To Heaven So The Father Could Send
The Holy Spirit

As aforementioned, the term *gospel* is best translated into *good* news. When considering the title, I envision news that would cause my life to be invigorated by provoking restoration of hope during turbulent times. So far we've covered three major points of the good news, inclusive of:

Point #1: We now know that Jesus *Came,* to the Earth with a special purpose as promised by God

Point #2: We now know that Jesus *Went,* to be both flogged and crucified on our behalf so we can embrace the provisions of God

Point #3: We now know that Jesus *Came* back again in the same physical body which was devastated and tortured to truly defeat death.

I would advocate that what was accomplished in the three areas above is GOOD NEWS! In fact, there are some who would stop at Point #3 as the complete gospel of Jesus. For many, the most important aspect of the gospel is that Jesus died for our sins and was resurrected. Although salvation after our earthly death is a marvelous gift, we are still missing one pivotal area of provision given through the sacrifice of Jesus the Messiah. What could be so important to warrant a conversation subsequent to Point #3? I'm glad you asked. The provision allotted by this next and final point involves Jesus' fulfillment to release the Holy Spirit, promised by his FATHER. Therefore: Point #4 Jesus *Went* to heaven in physical body but did not leave us alone. He sent the Holy Spirit, to empower, guide and counsel us.

Throughout Jesus' time on Earth, He told the disciples there were many things they did not understand, but to rejoice since his FATHER was sending the Holy Spirit to guide and empower them during their time on Earth. As you will learn in this chapter, the disciples were once a group of faithless and scared young men. However, once they came in to contact with the Holy Spirit, they were transformed into the persevering men of faith who would spread the gospel of Jesus with conviction and prowess until the end of their days.

Questions for the Heart

Your answers to these questions are not meant to be criticized, rather, they should be analyzed. Use this section to get a gauge of where you current knowledge and heart are by answering honestly. Be sure to write each answer on your notepad.

1) Have you ever heard of the Holy Spirit? If so, what do you know about Him?

2) Explain your familiarity with the Holy Spirit's work in the life Jesus?

3) Do you believe the heart of Jesus was for us to simply believe in him, die and go to Heaven? What do you believe His purpose for Believers was/is?

4) Do you believe GOD has a special purpose for you during your time on Earth? In short, what do you think that is? How far have you come to fulfilling your purpose on Earth?

5) Do you believe GOD not only created you with a purpose, but has equipped you with gifts and abilities to fulfill it? Can you identify how The Holy Spirit equipped Jesus' Disciples/Apostles?

The Ten Learning Steps

The Ten Learning Steps have been provided as a guide to help you make the most of each Study Scripture. Carefully focus on each Learning Step throughout this chapter to make the most of this endeavor.

1. For those who are willing, pray to GOD, in the name of Jesus for HIS Truth to be revealed to you.
2. Carefully read the Study Scripture at least 3 times, focusing on each minute detail.
3. Locate (online or hard copy) the Study Scripture in an amplified bible to discover the particulars of its content.
4. On a dedicated notepad, transcribe important thoughts derived from your initial glance. Ensure to notate portions of the Study Scripture which have the greatest relevance to you.
5. Do your best to answer the Investigative Questions section without referencing the Study Scripture.
6. Check or complete the Investigative Questions section by using the corresponding Study Scripture.
7. Record findings, questions and additions to your dedicated notepad.
8. Insert the location of each Study Scripture in your phone, tablet or notepad for future reference and memorization.
9. If possible, discuss your questions and comments with spiritual leaders, mentors, or friends who can guide you through this study.
10. As led, pray for clarity regarding areas of apprehension and ask GOD for deeper understanding.

Study Scripture: Luke 3:15-16, 21-22

"15As the people were in expectation, and all were questioning in their hearts concerning John, whether he might be the Christ, 16 John answered them all, saying, "I baptize you with water, but he who is mightier than I is coming, the strap of whose sandals I am not worthy to untie. He will baptize you with the Holy Spirit and fire. 21 Now when all the people were baptized, and when Jesus also had been baptized and was praying, the heavens were opened, 22 and the Holy Spirit descended on him in bodily form, like a dove; and a voice came from heaven, "You are my beloved Son; with you I am well pleased.""

<u>Shedding Light on Luke 3</u>

Although not entirely necessary, I would like to take a moment to point out the biblical accuracy of this Study Scripture. In the beginning of Luke 3— a practicing doctor— tells us this scripture is snapshotted when the affairs of the empire had been in the hands of Tiberius for over fifteen years. Through cross-referencing data we know Tiberius took office in 11 A.D. Therefore the events in this scripture took place in roughly 26 A.D. This ultimately puts Jesus on the cross around 30 AD. Again, I only emphasize this point to provide you with confidence in the reliability of the scriptures.

Another little known fact is that John the Baptist was born just a few months before his cousin, who is none other than Jesus Christ. John's father also received the announcement of his son by the angel Gabriel, just as Jesus' father did concerning his birth. John was a Jewish priest married to Elizabeth, a woman of elderly age. This also makes the birth of John the Baptist nothing other than supernatural. Gabriel tells John's Father Zachariah that his son will be filled with the Holy Spirit from his mother's womb and that he will turn the hearts of the people back to GOD.

The time period of John's ministry mentioned in the Study Scripture was foretold by the prophet Isaiah, hundreds of years earlier when he said, *"The voice of one crying in the wilderness: Prepare the way of the Lord; make His paths straight. Every valley shall be filled and every mountain and hill brought low; the crooked places shall be made straight and the rough ways smooth; and all flesh shall see the salvation of GOD"* (Isaiah 40:3-5).

John, specially gifted by GOD, pronounced his famous message, *"Prepare the way of the Lord"* (Isaiah 40:3). By this, John meant things for the people of GOD would soon be set right. It was a chance for them to prepare their hearts. After the execution of John the Baptist, Jesus clarifies his adoration for his cousin. This happened as he exhorted that John's efforts were not in vain since the lame walked, the blind could see, people were being cleansed from demonic influence, and the gospel was being told to the poor.

Investigative Questions

1. Verse 15 of the Study Scripture states that there were many in expectation and questioned whether John was the Christ. Based on what you've learned in the previous chapters of this book, why were the people in expectation for the Christ?

_____

_____

_____

_____

_____

_____

_____

_____

_____

_____

_____

2. How does John describe the Christ when the people ask if He is the one that they were waiting for *(v. 16)*?

_____

_____

_____

_____

_____

_____

_____

3. What does John say regarding the difference between his baptisms and those Jesus Christ will perform *(vs. 16)*?

_____

_____

_____

_____

_____

_____

_____

_____

4. What event occurred when Jesus was baptized by John *(v. 22)*?

_____

_____

_____

_____

_____

_____

_____

_____

_____

_____

_____

_____

5. In your opinion, why did the Holy Spirit descend like a dove upon Jesus *(vs 22)*?

_____

_____

_____

_____

_____

_____

_____

Study Scripture: Acts 1:1-9

"¹In the first book, O Theophilus, I have dealt with all that Jesus began to do and teach, ² until the day when he was taken up, after he had given commands through the Holy Spirit to the apostles whom he had chosen. ³ He presented himself alive to them after his suffering by many proofs, appearing to them during forty days and speaking about the kingdom of GOD. ⁴ And while staying with them he ordered them not to depart from Jerusalem, but to wait for the promise of the Father, which, he said, "you heard from me; ⁵ for John baptized with water, but you will be baptized with the Holy Spirit not many days from now."⁶ So when they had come together, they asked him, "Lord, will you at this time restore the kingdom to Israel?" ⁷ He said to them, "It is not for you to know times or seasons that the Father has fixed by his own authority. ⁸ But you will receive power when the Holy Spirit has come upon you, and you will be my witnesses in Jerusalem and in all Judea and Samaria, and to the end of the earth." ⁹ And when he had said these things, as they were looking on, he was lifted up, and a cloud took him out of their sight."

Shedding Light on Acts 1

Luke began his book, which we call the *Acts of the Apostles* or simply *Acts*, by picking up his story where it ended in his gospel. The gospel of Luke described Jesus' work in Galilee, Judea, as well as Jerusalem; the book ultimately ended with his death and resurrection.

The Book of Acts represents over one fourth of the New Testament and provides us with a detailed account of the radical transformation which took place in the hearts of the disciples after the resurrection and ascension of Jesus. It is centered upon the growth of the church and the spread of the gospel from Jerusalem to important cities of the Roman Empire—even to Rome itself.

Acts spans a period of about 30 years and takes us up to about 61 A.D. with Paul in Rome waiting to appear before Caesar Nero. It was the same Nero who began his infamous persecutions of Christians in 64 A.D. The Book of Acts provides history of the persistent opposition against the Gospel by the Jewish and Roman people. One of the greatest and most frequent problems the New Testament church had to deal with was the opposition of the Jews, who resisted the Gospel, and the mystics who sought to pervert it. The Gospel of Luke (and other Gospels) describes the roots of this opposition, which began as a resistance to Jesus' actions and teachings. The Book of Acts reflects how this opposition continued against the gospel and the early church after the death, burial, and resurrection of our Jesus.

What Paul does theologically in the book of Romans, Luke does historically in the Book of Acts. In the first chapter of his gospel, Luke told us that during his research he *carefully investigated everything from the beginning* (Luke 1:3). We would never understand the nature of the problems that faced the first Believers apart from The Book of Acts.

Investigative Questions

1. By which method did Jesus give commands to the disciples after His departure *(v. 2)*?

_____

_____

_____

_____

_____

_____

_____

_____

_____

_____

_____

2. How long did Jesus stay with His disciples after He resurrected *(v. 3)*?

_____

_____

_____

_____

_____

_____

_____

_____

_____

_____

_____

3. Why did Jesus command His disciples not to leave Jerusalem? In your opinion, what does this signify about the importance of that event *(v. 4-5)* ?

_____

_____

_____

_____

_____

_____

_____

_____

_____

4. Based on this scripture, explain why you believe Jesus continued to emphasize the Holy Spirit to His disciples *(v. 8)*?

_____

_____

_____

_____

_____

_____

_____

_____

_____

5. Jesus emphasized The Holy Spirit to his disciples. Do you think he would still prescribe partnering with the Holy Spirit to his modern day disciples? Why or why not?

_____

_____

_____

_____

_____

_____

_____

_____

_____

_____

_____

_____

_____

Study Scripture: Acts 2:1-11

"¹When the day of Pentecost arrived, they were all together in one place. ² And suddenly there came from heaven a sound like a mighty rushing wind, and it filled the entire house where they were sitting. ³ And divided tongues as of fire appeared to them and rested on each one of them. ⁴ And they were all filled with the Holy Spirit and began to speak in other tongues as the Spirit gave them utterance. ⁵ Now there were dwelling in Jerusalem Jews, devout men from every nation under heaven. ⁶ And at this sound the multitude came together, and they were bewildered, because each one was hearing them speak in his own language. ⁷ And they were amazed and astonished, saying, "Are not all these who are speaking Galileans? ⁸ And how is it that we hear, each of us in his own native language? ⁹ Parthians and Medes and Elamites and residents of Mesopotamia, Judea and Cappadocia, Pontus and Asia, ¹⁰ Phrygia and Pamphylia, Egypt and the parts of Libya belonging to Cyrene, and visitors from Rome, ¹¹ both Jews and proselytes, Cretans and Arabians—we hear them telling in our own tongues the mighty works of GOD."

Shedding Light on Acts 2

Although unable to elaborate in content of this book, I would like to point out a powerful symbiotic relationship between events noted in the Torah (Old Testament) and the Book of Acts. The events of which I am referring to are centered on the day of Pentecost—also known as Shavuot in Hebrew. Most Christians are unaware that Pentecost (Shavuot) predated the New Testament experience and began with Moses and the Jewish people. I am zealously against any gospel which caters to the replacement of the Jewish people with Christians, also known as "replacement theology" .

On the Day of Pentecost around 1300 B.C., GOD gave His Law, the Ten Commandments or the "Old Covenant", to Moses on Mount Sinai accompanied by thunder and lightning. Over 1,000 years later, on the day of Pentecost, GOD sent down His Holy Spirit, like a rushing mighty wind so the New Covenant of life would be established. When the giving of the Law commenced, 3000 people died due to acts of disobedience. When the giving of the Holy Spirit occurred, on the very same day, over 1000 years later, over 3000 people accepted Jesus as their Savior due to their encounter with The Holy Spirit (Acts 2:41).

Why did GOD give the Law knowing HIS people could not uphold it? No one can speak entirely on behalf of the heart of GOD. However, for the purposes of this book I would say He did it to set a standard of morality. The Jewish people had been subject to many rulers and ideologies. GOD wanted to establish a set of laws which would encourage people to have better behavior and connection with Him. Additionally, when people would abide by the Law, it served as a mark or distinction between them as the people of GOD and the rest of the world.

It is important to understand that the Jewish people were the first to embrace and abide by a monotheistic standard. They were the first to believe there was only one GOD who reigned. This is in contrast to the competing worldviews that supported a belief in multiple GODs. The First Covenant, known as *the Law* or *Old Covenant*, from the first Pentecost was only given as a precursor of things to come. As promised, on the day of Pentecost mentioned in the book of Acts, GOD delivered His new and final covenant through the Holy Spirit. This "New Covenant" was greater than the "Old Covenant" because rather than judging according to sin, GOD would receive mankind based on his acceptance and following of His Son Jesus Christ (Jeremiah 31:33).

Investigative Questions

1. On what day or holiday were the disciples gathered together *(v.1)*?

_____
_____
_____
_____
_____
_____
_____
_____

2. What "suddenly" appeared as they were in the house that they were in? What are your thoughts on that event *(v.2)*?

_____
_____

_____
_____
_____
_____
_____
_____
_____
_____
_____

3. What happened to the disciples at that moment *(v. 4)*?

_____
_____
_____
_____
_____
_____
_____

4. What sound did the multitude of foreigners dwelling outside of the house hear *(v. 6)*?

_____
_____
_____
_____
_____
_____
_____
_____
_____

5. What was the interpretation of what was spoken by those in the house *(v. 11)*?

_____
_____
_____
_____
_____
_____
_____
_____
_____
_____

6. How do you believe this event impacted those who were outside of the house? Could this have been done without the Holy Spirit?

_____

_____

_____

_____

_____

_____

_____

_____

_____

_____

_____

"9 But there was a man named Simon, who had previously practiced magic in the city and amazed the people of Samaria, saying that he himself was somebody great. 10 They all paid attention to him, from the least to the greatest, saying, "This man is the power of GOD that is called Great."11 And they paid attention to him because for a long time he had amazed them with his magic. 12 But when they believed Philip as he preached good news about the kingdom of GOD and the name of Jesus Christ, they were baptized, both men and women. 13 Even Simon himself believed, and after being baptized he continued with Philip. And seeing signs and great miracles performed, he was amazed.

14 Now when the Apostles at Jerusalem heard that Samaria had received the word of GOD, they sent to them Peter and John, 15 who came down and prayed for them that they might receive the Holy Spirit, 16 for he had not yet fallen on any of them, but they had only been baptized in the name of the Lord Jesus. 17 Then they laid their hands on them and they received the Holy Spirit. 18 Now when Simon saw that the Holy Spirit was given by the laying on of the Apostles hands he offered the money, 19 saying, "give me this power also, so that anyone on whom I lay my hands may receive the Holy Spirit. 20 But Peter said to him," May your silver perish with you because you though you could obtain the gift of GOD with money."

Shedding Light on Acts 8

Chapter 8 of Acts opens with the murder of Stephen, a mature Believer in Jesus, by a mob of Jewish leaders. This was a great blow to the enthusiasm of the early church. Amongst this gang of antagonists was Saul of Tarsus, later to be known as Paul. This Paul would later become the writer of one-third of the New Testament. As a Christian leader, Stephen exemplified being filled with the Spirit. As an evangelist, he possessed a boldness and an eloquence which caused him to be admired by many. The chapter states that after his death, *"devout men carried Stephen to his burial, and made great lamentation over him"* (Acts 8:2).

Unfortunately, this atrocity was only the beginning of trouble for the followers of Jesus. The leaders who stoned Stephen turned their attention towards the remaining group of Christians in Jerusalem. Angry Jewish mobs led by Saul of Tarsus conducted house-to-house searches for believers and throwing those they found into jail. Fear of imprisonment and death drove many out of the city. Despite the circumstances, the once fearful Apostles, boldly remained in Jerusalem and continued to spread the gospel throughout the region.

Within a short time of being selected by the Apostles, Philip—not the disciple of Jesus, but a former deacon— brought the message of the gospel to three new regions. He was the first known Christian leader who ministered the gospel to the Samaritans.

The Bible tell us that everywhere Philip went, he had the special gifting and power of the Holy Spirit with him. In the city of Samaria, he preached with great authority and performed astounding miracles. The lame and paralyzed were healed. The possessed were delivered from demonic control. When the Samaritans heard Philip and saw the miracles, they all believed with joy. Many were baptized in water as an outward confession of their belief in Jesus.

Investigative Questions

1. How did people perceive Simon in the beginning of the scripture *(vv. 9-10)?*

_____
_____
_____
_____
_____
_____
_____
_____
_____
_____

2. What did the people, including Simon, do at the message of Phillip? What did they see Philip perform *(vv. 12-13)?*

_____
_____
_____
_____

_____
_____
_____
_____
_____
_____
_____
_____

3. Why did the Apostles go to see the people of Samaria when Stephen left *(vv. 14-16)?*

_____
_____
_____
_____
_____
_____
_____

4. In your opinion, what does the apostles excursion towards the people of Samaria reflect of their emphasis on the Holy Spirit? Why couldn't the people be settled with water baptism alone?

_____
_____
_____
_____
_____
_____
_____
_____

5. How did the apostle release the Holy Spirit to the people of Samaria *(v. 18)?*

_____
_____
_____
_____
_____
_____
_____
_____
_____
_____

6. According to the Study Scripture, the baptism of the Holy Spirit was not solely for Jesus, the apostles, or those in their ministry. It was for all to receive. Do you believe the Holy Spirit is still needed today?

_____

_____

_____

_____

_____

_____

_____

_____

_____

Chapter 5: He Went
Establishing the Flogging and Crucifixion of Jesus
Day 27

Day 27
Chapter 6 He Came
Establishing the First Coming of
Jesus

Establishing the First Coming of Jesus Through Key Points

Despite what many believe, Jesus was not simply a good person who tried to make life better for others. Jesus is unique in that His birth and mission was established and prophetically recorded long before His arrival. There were no legitimate claims pertaining to the birth of other known spiritual leaders. While observing the circumstances surrounding the birth of Jesus, Christians can rejoice knowing He came to earth intentionally to restore our original relationship with GOD. We can praise GOD for fulfilling His promises, while resting in complete confidence He will always be faithful to do what He has declared. Let us review and introduce a couple new key points prophetically fulfilled to qualify Jesus as the promised Savior:

1. Jesus was from Bethlehem

Many of the Jews from Jesus' day were aware the Messiah was to come from Bethlehem (Matthew 2:3-6). For most, their understanding was based upon a scripture from the Jewish prophet Micah:

> *But you, Bethlehem Ephrathah, though you are little among the*
> *thousands of Judah, yet out of you shall come forth to Me the*
> *One to be Ruler in Israel, whose goings forth are from of old,*
> *from everlasting.* (Micah 5:2)

At the time there were two Bethlehems. One Bethlehem was located near Ephrathah in Judea, and the other to the North near the tribe of Zebulun. Micah's prophecy is precise stating that Jesus would be born in Bethlehem of Ephrathah. The location of His birth was confirmed in Matthew 2:1.

2. Jesus Was Born of a Virgin

There is a remarkable prophecy called the *Emmanuel Prophecy*, which foretells the unique birth of Jesus by a virgin by stating, "Behold, the virgin shall conceive and bear a Son, and shall call His name Immanuel" (Isaiah 7:14).

Before Jesus was born, an angel appeared to his father Joseph in a dream. The angel informed him that his fiancé, Mary, was expecting a child. This was mentioned by the prophet Isaiah. Moreover the child was not conceived by man, but by the Spirit of GOD (Matthew 1:18-23; Luke 1:26-35). In one sense, one must imagine Joseph was relieved to hear Mary had been faithful all along. On another hand, as a husband and father, I still must wonder how Joseph reconciled the event. Nonetheless, the prophecy was miraculously fulfilled and Jesus entered the earth as prescribed by GOD.

3. Jesus was a Descendant of Abraham and David

In Galatians 3:8, Paul teaches us of the promise made to Abraham, "In you all the nations of the earth shall be blessed" (Genesis 12:3; Genesis 18:18; Genesis 22:18). This was also a reference to the coming Savior. This promise was later repeated to Abraham's son Isaac and then later passed on through Abraham's grandson Jacob (Genesis 26:4; Genesis 28:14). Several hundred years later the future Savior was prophesied to come through Jesse, the father of David and king of the tribe of Judah:

There shall come forth a Rod [Shoot] from the stem [stock] of Jesse, and a Branch shall grow out of His roots (Isaiah 11:1)

David was the son of Jesse from whom the Branch would arise from. Jesus of Nazareth would then appear roughly 30 generations later. In this amazing progression of prophecies, beginning 1,500 years before the Messiah came, we are told in precise terms what the human lineage of the Christ would be. The number of people who could have fulfilled this quota narrows greatly when limited to this family.

4. Jesus Was a Prophet Like Moses

Over 1400 years before Jesus, Moses gave prophecy concerning the coming Messiah. His prophecy was unique because it was tied directly to him, demonstrating Moses understood he was a foreshadow of the coming Savior who would come.

The Lord said to me: 'What they say is good. I will raise up for them a prophet like you from among their brothers; I will put my words in his mouth, and he will tell them everything I command him'. (Deuteronomy 18:17-18)

Moses described the denotation for the Savior by emphasizing their similarities. No other prophet in the Scriptures shared as many similarities with Jesus as did Moses. One interesting example is that as infants, evil kings would threaten both Jesus and Moses. Yet, both would be supernaturally protected from harm (Exodus 1:14-2:10; Matthew 2:13-16). Additionally similar to Moses, Jesus was also a leader, teacher, law-giver , deliverer, and miracle worker (John 15:12 and Matthew 22:37-39). Both also healed lepers, acted as covenant mediators, and performed duties as priests (Numbers 12:10-15; Matthew 8:1-3; Luke 17:12-14, Exodus 33:7-11; 1 Timothy 2:5).

The Prophesied Coming of Jesus Was For You

The uniqueness of Christianity rests upon the uniqueness of Jesus Christ. He entered the world in the timing, ancestry, and geographical location foretold hundreds of years before His coming. Therefore, Jesus' birth stands alone in history. By the miraculous work of the Holy Spirit, Mary the virgin gave birth to Jesus who was both GOD and Man. Because of His unique birth, Jesus could bypass the curse of sin to uniquely qualify as the sinless Savior. He was born to go to the cross and die as the slain, sacrificial Lamb of GOD. This great feat should give you confidence in Jesus and the promise of the reconciliation with GOD that He brings. Jesus was sent solely for you to experience life with GOD. NOW THAT'S GOOD NEWS!

Chapter 6: He Went
Establishing the Flogging and Crucifixion of Jesus
Day 28

Establishing the Flogging and Crucifixion of Jesus Through Key Points

Biblical prophecies regarding the crucifixion of Jesus were especially unique. Interestingly, when the execution of Jesus was prophesied in Psalm 22, death-by-crucifixion would have been unknown to the writers who lived in modern day Palestine. The acknowledgement of supernatural phenomena such as darkness, earthquakes, and the opening of the graves surrounded the crucifixion story. Upon witnessing Jesus on the cross and the events of that day, the Roman centurion who witnessed hundreds die from crucifixion proclaimed, *"Truly this was the Son of GOD"* (Matthew 27:54;Mark 15:39;Luke 23:47) Hopefully, you have come to the same conclusion through your study of the compelling evidence found in this book. Let us review and introduce a couple of new key points that were prophetically fulfilled to qualify Jesus as the promised Savior:

1. Jesus Was Crucified

"They pierced My hands and My feet" (Psalms 22:16). This statement was written 1,000 years before the event which fulfilled in John 20:25-27. Perhaps even more remarkable, this prophecy described execution which would not come into practice until the Romans adopted crucifixion as punishment some 800 years later.

2. The Body of Jesus was Pierced

Long before Jesus came to the Earth, the prophet Zechariah foretold of His piercing by saying , "They will look on Me whom they pierced" (Zechariah 12:10).

Jesus' disciple John confirms the event occurred as he wrote, "One of the soldiers pierced His side with a spear, and immediately blood and water came out" (John 19:34). John also informs readers that he was an eyewitness to the event and verifies that it was fulfillment of prophecy (John 19:35).

3. Jesus Did Not Suffer a Broken Bone

In another profound prophecy the psalmist prophesied that Jesus would not suffer a broken bone as he also wrote, "He guards all his bones; not one of them is broken." (Psalms 34:20). The disciple John tells us, "Then the soldiers came and broke the legs of the first and of the other who was crucified with Him. But when they came to Jesus and saw He was already dead, they did not break His legs" (John 19:32-33). John verifies this as a prophecy , which was fulfilled in the book of John: "For these things were done that the Scripture should be fulfilled, 'Not one of His bones shall be broken'" (John 19:36).

4. Jesus was Executed With Criminals

The prophet Isaiah describes in detail hundreds of years later that, the Savior would be killed in the midst of common criminals as he said, "And He was numbered with the transgressors" (Isaiah 53:21). In Matthew 27:38, the former tax collector and disciple of Jesus tells us "two robbers were crucified with Him, one on the right and another on the left".

5. Jesus was Betrayed by a Trusted Friend

The betrayal of Jesus by Judas, one of His disciples, was prophesied:

Psalms 41:9: "Even my own familiar friend in whom I trusted, who ate my bread, has lifted up his heel against me."

Jesus proclaims this prophecy to be fulfilled when He gives Judas the piece of bread in John 13:18 and John 13:26.The price of the betrayal would be 30 pieces of silver. The 30 pieces of silver paid to Judas for the betrayal of Jesus (Matthew 26:14-15) is understood to have been prophesied in Zechariah 11:12: "So they weighed out for my wages thirty pieces of silver."

The Flogging and Crucifixion of Jesus Was For You

Over two millennia ago Jesus was beaten, whipped, flogged, spit upon, mocked, and scourged with a lead-tipped whip. His Beard was ripped off His Face. During His crucifixion He endured hours of humiliation by having to hang on a cross between two thieves—bleeding to death, nearly naked. He was falsely accused by the temple and abandoned by His friends. After graphically reminding us of the flogging endured by

Jesus, Peter joyfully proclaims it was by these same stripes in which we were healed (1 Peter 2:24).

I must reiterate that the word *healed* is the Greek word "iaomai", referencing *"physical healing"*. The Greek word was derived from a medical term used to describe the physical healing or curing of the human body. In essence, Peter is saying that *by the stripes of Jesus, we are physically healed.*

Are you a Christian who does not believe GOD still heals today? Believe it or not, you are not alone. There is a group of Christians known as *cessationists* who believe the supernatural power of GOD ceased working through man, subsequent to the canonization or compiling of the Bible. Considering this to be an introductory book, I wish not to delve too far into this matter. However, it would be ill served if I did not at least address it.

The pivotal verse for cessation theory is found in the book of Corinthians:

"Love never fails. But where there are prophecies, they will cease; where there are tongues, they will be stilled; where there is knowledge, it will pass away. For we know in part and we prophesy in part, but when completeness comes, what is in part disappears."(1 Corinthians 13:1-3)

Those subscribe to theory of cessation prescribe the term *"completeness"*, to mean when the bible is *compiled* or *completed*. Was the Apostle Paul referring to the compilation of the Bible as a sign that GOD retracting supernatural power from His people? In the same letter, as a benchmark Paul explains that the gifts of GOD will continue to exist until the second coming of Jesus Christ (1 Corinthians 1:7). Personally, I would adopt this to be the benchmark when deciphering the term *completeness* as it refers to the context of 1 Corinthians 13:1-3. I digress.

My humble rendition? Surely, Paul was highlighting the significance and supremacy of love over spiritual gifts. In other words, the Christians living in Corinth were cautioned against over-rating spiritual gifts. We can safely assert that GOD is far more concerned with the state of our hearts rather than our deeds. Good hearts seamlessly produce good deeds. Furthermore, one's operation in supernatural gifts does not necessarily equate to good heart.

Please allow me to provide you with one last and simple thought before navigating away from the topic of cessationism. It is impossible to read about the life of Jesus without running into supernatural events. Jesus yielded His power over sickness and wicked spiritual forces. Yes, by wicked spiritual forces I am referring to demons. When reading through the Gospels you will notice the continued mention of people being demonized, who ultimately where delivered and healed by Jesus. Please read the following verse: *"When the evening was come, they brought unto him many that were possessed with devils: and he cast out the spirits with his word, and healed all that were sick: That it might be fulfilled which was spoken by Isaiah the prophet, saying, Himself took our infirmities, and bare our sicknesses."* (Matthew 8:16-17)

The Apostle Matthew seemed to believe "by His stripes we are healed" should be taken literally. On that note, I would like to give you a series of questions to consider:

1) Do you believe the Bible in its depiction of demonic spirits in the time of Jesus? (Remember Jesus mentioned and demonstrated power over them throughout His ministry).

2) Assuming demonic spirits existed, would they have disappeared upon compilation of the modern day bible? If so, what would cause them to?

3) Do you believe we live in a world which is relatively evil? Is it possible demonic spirits are still in operation?

4) Assuming you believe evil spirits are still active, do you believe it is the Heart of GOD to leave you stranded, without deliverance from sickness and oppression?

5) Do you believe GOD has given you the Bible, not to receive healing, but "only" to read about the people Jesus healed during His time on Earth? If so, does that sound like "good news?"

Hopefully my line of questioning provoked you to study and seek clarity through prayer. Beloved, I pray that the eyes of your heart will see that Jesus hasn't changed His mind on your deliverance and healing (Hebrews 13:8). He wants you to be set free. The punishment Jesus took was for you to be healed and have peace, even in adversity. I have been healed by GOD from what should have been a chronic, life-long disease. Beloved, the flogging and crucifixion of Jesus was for you to be whole. Now, that's good news!

Chapter 8 He Came
Establishing the Physical Resurrection of Jesus
Day 29

Establishing the Physical Resurrection of Jesus Through Key Points

The indispensable issue of Christianity is the question, *"Did Jesus Christ rise from the grave?"* Was the resurrection of Jesus an actual bodily resurrection or merely a spiritual manifestation of some sort? Since the day Jesus rose from the dead, doubters have tried to deny the reality of His resurrection because a genuine resurrection proves His deity. Christians must be fully persuaded that the resurrection was actual event, because salvation itself depends upon the reality of the Lord physically rising from the dead. When presented with the facts, it is difficult not to admit the resurrection is historically based. Let us review and introduce a couple new key points prophetically fulfilled to qualify Jesus as the promised Savior:

1. Jesus Predicted His Own Death and Resurrection

The Bible records, "From that time Jesus began to show His disciples that He must go to Jerusalem, and suffer many things ... and be killed, and be raised up on the third day" (Matthew 16:21). Even though His followers did not understand what He was telling them they remembered His words and recorded them.

2. Jesus Appeared to Marry Magdalene After His Resurrection

When Mary Magdalene and the others went to the tomb to prepare the body of Jesus, they were told by the angel, "He is not here; for He is risen, as He said. Come, see the place where the Lord lay. And go quickly and tell His disciples that He is risen from the dead" (Matthew 28:6–7). These women were told Jesus was raised from the dead. This implies an actual physical resurrection.

3. Jesus Appeared on the Road to Emmaus

Jesus appeared to two disciples on the road to Emmaus (Mark 16:12–13; Luke 24:13–31). These two disciples walked and talked with Him along the way. In the evening, they sat down to eat. As they were handed the bread, they recognized Him.

The scripture says, "Then their eyes were opened and they knew Him; and He vanished from their sight" (Luke 24:31).

4. The Tomb of Jesus is Empty

The authorities could have easily put this entire issue to rest by merely producing the dead body of Jesus. There is no historical documentation, from either the Bible or other ancient documents, which suggests that a body could be produced. Enemies of Christianity through the ages would relish the evidence of a body in the tomb. Such evidence would be the death knell of Christianity.

The best argument raised by those who opposed Christ was that His disciples stole His body while the soldiers who guarded the tomb were asleep. It is unrealistic to expect the once fleeing disciples to evade or subdue the Roman guards at the tomb, break the seal, roll away the stone, and steal the body of Jesus. Besides, what would be their motive? The Bible describes the disciples scattering in fear, because they had not yet grasped that Jesus must die and rise from the dead. From their standpoint, what could they possibly benefit from engaging in such an endeavor?

Perhaps the strongest rejection of this argument is their bold witness after Jesus' resurrection. These men would die for their faith after coming into contact with the risen Jesus. Never did any of the disciples deny Christ, even in the midst of terrible trials and ordeals. If they had stolen the body, would they really be willing to die to conceal this act?

Finally, one of the most compelling evidences for the empty tomb was the action of the chief priests and elders when told of the empty tomb. Instead of producing the body, they merely told the soldiers to say the disciples had stolen the body. Matthew 28:21-13 reads, "When they had assembled with the elders and consulted together, they gave a large sum of money to the soldiers, saying, 'Tell them, "His disciples came at night and stole Him away while we slept"'.

One thing is for sure. If they could have produced the Body of Jesus, Christianity would never have left the stage of infancy. Notice that even the best argument of the day contradicts itself. How could the soldiers know who stole the body do so if they were asleep as the alleged theft occurred?

5. Jesus Gave a Sermon After His Resurrection

Jesus Christ appeared consistently to many of His followers. On one occasion, He gathered His remaining eleven disciples on a mountain in Galilee and gave them His Great Commission. He said, "Go therefore and make disciples of all the nations, baptizing them in the name of the Father and the Son and the Holy Spirit, teaching them to observe all that I commanded you; and lo, I am with you always" (Matthew 28:19,20). Later, the book of Acts records that on the Mount of Olives, He admonished His disciples to wait in Jerusalem until they were filled with the Holy Spirit and then to take His message to Jerusalem, Judea, Samaria and to the ends of the world (Acts 1:4,5,8).

The Physical Resurrection Was For You

The resurrection proved Jesus Christ was divine. The fact Jesus Christ died on the cross does not prove He is GOD. Jesus proved His deity by fulfilling the prophecies of His death and by His return from the grave. The resurrection proved Christ's power to forgive sin. The Apostle Paul said, "If Christ has not been raised, your faith is worthless; you are still in your sins" (1 Corinthians 15:17). By rising from the dead, Jesus proved His authority and power to break the bondages of sin and death, ensuring that you are GOD'S possession—if you accept His gift of salvation. His physical resurrection guarantees your eternity. Now, that's Good News!

Chapter 8: He Went

Establishing the Ascension of Jesus & Release of The Holy Spirit

Day 30

Day 30
Chapter 8 He Went
Establishing the Ascension of Jesus
& the Release of The Holy Spirit

Establishing the Ascension of Jesus & the Release of the Holy Spirit Through Key Points

Contrary to other religious leaders, Jesus provided His follower with supernatural support in His physical absence. The Holy Spirit came to glorify Christ and to lead Believers into all truth. The Holy Spirit is GOD. He is not an "it", nor is He simply a "divine influence". He is a supernatural person possessing a will, intellect, and emotions. He is the GOD'S Spirit, with all the attributes of deity. Through the obedience of Jesus, the Holy Spirit could be sent to "live in" Believers of Christ. Let us review and introduce two new key points prophetically fulfilled to qualify Jesus as the promised Savior:

1. Jesus Predicted the Release of The Holy Spirit

Towards the end of the earthly ministry of Jesus, He advised the disciples of His powerful replacement Who would come. The disciples were grieved that their leader would one day have to leave. Jesus sought to give them hope as He shared, "All this I have spoken while still with you. But the Counselor, the Holy Spirit, whom the Father will send in my name, will teach you all things and will remind you of everything I have said to you" (John 14:25-26). Furthermore, He went on to say, "He will bring glory to me by taking from what is mine and making it known to you" (John 16:14).

As you've read in previous chapters, the Holy Spirit did come—and with quite the impact. The Holy Spirit brought the same power, which Jesus had and imparted it to the apostles. As such, every chapter within the book of Acts is filled with miracles committed by the Apostles on behalf of Jesus.

2. The Physical Body of Jesus Was Raised to Heaven

A thousand years before the Savior's birth, the psalmist prophesied the ascension of Jesus when He announced the Lord's enthronement at the Father's right hand (Psalm 110:1). Though the disciples struggled with the concept of Jesus' death, He told them plainly that he was going back to the Father (John 14:12). While on trial before the Jewish Sanhedrin, Jesus announced to the high priest that He would be "sitting at the right hand of Power" (Matthew 26:64). His ascension was one of the tests of Christ's prophetic credibility. The ascension of Jesus allowed the Holy Spirit to dwell in Believers, by taking the place of His bodily presence, so they could continue what He had done while on Earth (John 14:16-17; 16:5-7).

3. Jesus Sent the Holy Spirit at Pentecost (Shavuot)

Just before the resurrected Jesus is taken up into heaven (Acts 1), He tells the disciples about the Father's promised gift of the Holy Spirit, which will soon be given to them in a powerful baptism. He tells them to wait in Jerusalem until they receive the gift of the Holy Spirit, which will empower them to go out into the world and be His witnesses.

A few days later, on the *Day of Pentecost*, the disciples were all together when the sound of a mighty wind comes down from heaven, with tongues of fire resting on them. The Bible says, "All of them were filled with the Holy Spirit and began to speak in other tongues as the Spirit enabled them" (Acts 2:4). The crowds observed this event and heard them speaking in different languages. Newly filled with the Holy Spirit, Peter preached the Gospel of the Kingdom of GOD and 3000 people accepted the message of Christ! That day, they were baptized and added to the family of GOD. What a day! I would like to reiterate Pentecost was an established Jewish Feast Day (Holiday) over 1,000 years before the Christian Pentecost of the Upper Room. Although, it was not known by the Greek name *"Pentecost"* rather it was called *"Feast of Weeks"* or *"Shavuot"* in Hebrew.

Jesus Ascended and Sent The Holy Spirit For You

I am concerned with where the state of the Body of Christ is today. This is particularly because as I speak with what appear to be mature Believers, they have no concept of the purpose or works of the Holy Spirit. Considering how Jesus and His apostles centered their ministries on partnering with the Holy Spirit, I have a hard time embracing the fact that Christians are not placing more of a demand to learn more about Him.

Listen friend, nothing can take the place of the Holy Spirit's work in the life of the Believer. Through Him, we are *"heirs of GOD with Jesus Christ"* according to the Apostle Paul's writing in Romans 8:17. We who receive the Holy Spirit are infinitely richer than the wealthiest of the world, because what we possess is an eternal inheritance. By receiving the Holy Spirit I mean receiving Jesus so the Holy Spirit can live within you. This is where the determination of your eternity is found. Accepting Jesus into your heart is, however, different than receiving the baptism of the Holy Spirit.

Receiving Jesus and being baptized in water is a start, yet the baptism of the Holy Spirit should be the goal. Water baptism is only an outward sign that you are retiring your former life to follow GOD. Water baptism is beautiful. As a Pastor, I am often involved in the process for our congregation. Though it is a great milestone, which often leads to behavioral change, it was not the baptism for which Jesus was sent. Jesus Himself said, "John baptized with water, but in a few days you will be baptized with the Holy Spirit" (Acts 1:5). The baptism of Holy Spirit is a vital step for any Christian serious about maturing into who GOD called them to be. This baptism is essential for both knowing GOD and making Him known.

Often, Christians attempt to woo over potential converts with their intellectual monologues. For many, this is their preferred means because they have not received the Baptism of The Holy Spirit. Therefore, they lack the power and understanding necessary to operate within the nature of GOD. Without the baptism of the Holy Spirit, Believers are primarily operating out of their human consciousness. When a Believer receives the Holy Spirit they have the *opportunity* to think and operate like GOD. The lives of the apostles are the best case study for this transformation. They were once scared, abrasive and reliant upon their human understanding. In fact, they could not even comprehend the parables or scriptures regarding their leader Jesus. Once the Holy Spirit came upon them, that all changed. Beloved, I witness this very same shift among today's Believers regularly. The Holy Spirit brings them from fright to boldness, from doubt to faith, from disobedience to maturity.

When someone receives the Holy Spirit, they receive power to heal, prophesy, and communicate with GOD supernaturally (Gift of Tongues), just as Jesus promised. The Holy Spirit is responsible for leading you to the depths of GOD, away from immaturity.

In his first letter to the Corinthians, Paul tells them, it is the Holy Spirit who makes the invisible, visible and the unheard, heard by revealing the depth of GOD.

It is important for every Christian to understand and experience the Baptism of the Holy Spirit for themselves. Believers need the power which comes with the Baptism of the Spirit to do their part in continuing the supernatural ministry of Jesus Christ. Jesus promised the Believers that they would do greater works than He (John 14:12).

One of the best statements from Jesus is found in John 14:12 when He says, "Verily, verily, I say unto you, He that believeth on me, the works that I do shall he do also; and greater works than these shall he do; because I go unto my Father". I hope this statement excites you at least half as much as it does me. But, how can this be done unless the Holy Spirit is with us as He was with Jesus? The church today is in need of the Power , which only comes through the relationship and baptism of Holy Spirit.

Please allow me to close this chapter with a personal plea. Beloved, you can continue to read about the works of Jesus, or you can fulfill His heart by accepting the gift of the Holy Spirit and operating just as He did. This gift isn't tailored for the rich or studied. In fact, such status may make operating with the Holy Spirit more complicated. This is a gift for the meek and those who will seek Him like children.

If you are being convicted of your need to be baptized with the Holy Spirit, I would like to pray with you. Please repeat after me:

"Father in Heaven, I thank you for the gift of the Holy Spirit. I believe you sent Him to guide and empower me for your purpose. I am ready to begin my journey with you. I ask for forgiveness if I have said anything that may have grieved Him. I ask that you send the Holy Spirit into my life so that I am able to serve you with greater measure, in the Name of Jesus. Amen."

I believe if you have prayed that prayer, whole-heartedly, the Holy Spirit will come over your life at the right time. When He comes, you will receive the power, authority, and character of GOD as you draw closer to Jesus. Now, that sounds like Good News!

Proving Jesus Through Probability

What are the odds? Having spent my career in investment banking, I can't help but to determine a quantitative (number based) metric to establish the validity of representations.

By the term "odds", I am referring to a branch of mathematics which measures the likelihood that a given event will occur. Let us have a quick look at some interesting odds:

Being struck by lightning in a year = 7×10^5 or 1 in 700,000

Becoming president = 1×10^7 or 1 in 10,000,000

An asteroid landing on your house = 1.8×10^{14} or 1 in 180,000,000,000,000

As you can see, the probability of being struck by lightning, becoming president, or having an asteroid land on your house, progressively increases toward unimaginably slim probabilities. Now, let's turn our calculators over to the life of Jesus. Dr. Stoner, of Science Speaks, examines the probability that one man, Jesus Christ, could have fulfilled just 8 of the 300 prophecies pertaining to Him in the Bible. For Jesus to fulfill 8 of the common prophecies:

Jesus fulfills just 8 prophecies: 1×10^{28} or 1 in 10,000,000,000,000,000,000,000,000,000.

I could rest my case with the statement representation above. Yet, I will expound that the Tanach contains nearly "300" prophetic passages which describe the Savior in great detail. Among all, there are "60" major prophecies. The formula above only calculated "8". What are the chances of these prophecies being fulfilled in one person?

How should we interpret the numbers? Christ is unique among all who ever lived. He is unique in His supernatural nature, in His matchless character, and in His life and teaching. No other world teacher has claimed to be GOD. No other legitimate religious leader offered salvation by faith, apart from works, based on their ability to take away the sin and reconcile humanity back to GOD. Jesus Christ was exclusive in every way. From His complete deity, to His perfect humanity, from His miraculous conception to His supernatural ascension and release of the Holy Spirit, Jesus stands above all other religious or moral teachers. Now, how will you respond to this claim?

The Great Commission

Most Christians know that the Great Commission from Jesus to His followers said, *"All authority in heaven and on earth has been given to me. Go therefore and make disciples of all nations, baptizing them in the name of the Father and of the Son and of the Holy Spirit, teaching them to observe all that I have commanded you. And behold, I am with you always, to the end of the age"* (Matthew 28:18-2).

How exciting! When we represent Jesus Christ, we are representing the Savior who holds all power, wisdom, and authority. We have the ability to change everything when we partner Him. Jesus said, "I tell you the truth, anyone who has faith in me will do what I have been doing. He will do even greater things than these, because I am going to the Father" (John 14:12). This statement is all the more reason why we should be excited about going out and *demonstrating* the Gospel.

The big question is, do we believe this mandate is still prevalent today? Seemingly, we have gotten the idea that the early Christians were different from us in that they enjoyed a quality of life that is unattainable for us. On the contrary, it is a historical fact that the recipients of the Great Commission were ordinary working people, plagued by the same weaknesses which we experience. There are only two foundational principals that separate them from the majority of us. The first is, they actually believed Jesus was resurrected. The second is, they were filled and empowered by the Holy Spirit.

If more of us embraced the principals of true belief and the baptism of the Holy Spirit, we might be less cavalier about evangelism and discipleship. If we truly are followers impacted by Jesus, the desire to share our experience would evident. Is it possible to be the disciples GOD wants us to be without spreading the Good News of HIS Son's death and resurrection? Unlikely. On the bright side, the prescription for spiritual impotence is simple. We simply believe, go out and win people to Christ, then help them grow spiritually; that is fulfilling the Great Commission.

Disciple(s) vs. Convert(s)

Jesus said to go out and make disciples. For many in the church today, *making disciples* is synonymous with *making converts*. There is a huge difference between the two. To be a disciple one must be a convert, but to be a convert one does not have to be a disciple. Disciple, similar to the word "discipline", requires one to become a student of someone who has become mature in his or her faith. Jesus commanded and exemplified discipleship with his twelve disciples. In turn, the apostles paid it forward by repeating the effort with those brought into the Faith. Discipleship requires the mature Believer and the new *convert* to take active roles within the relationship. The end goal: That over time, the new Believer is guided to take on the character, power, and assignment of Jesus Christ.

Pay it Forward

It is possible Believers are missing the mark in achieving the Great Commission because so many of us have been taught how to be "saved" with minimal instruction on how we could become and make disciples. My prayer is you will use this study, not simply as an intellectual guide, but a tool to develop relationships. Use this book as a study guide when meeting with friends, hold studies at your home or church, while ensuring true companionship is involved. Jesus laughed, danced, and ate with His disciples regularly.

For you who consider yourself a convert, I pray GOD will open up doors for you to find someone to disciple you. For you who have been discipled, having reached a comfortable level of maturity, I pray you will find someone to disciple. Discipleship and relationship among Believers is essential to carrying the torch Jesus gave and touching the heart of GOD.

References

1 Derek Kidner, Genesis, An Introduction and Commentary, Inter-Varsity Press, p. 70.

3 Merrill F. Unger, Unger's Commentary on the Old Testament, Vol. I, p. 31.

4 Notes on Genesis 5:3, Ryrie Study Bible, Expanded Edition, 1995, p. 11.

6 Allen Ross, The Bible Knowledge Commentary, Old Testament, John F. Walvoord and Roy B. Zuck, Editors, p. 36.

7 For more information on this, see J. Dwight Pentecost's, Prophecy For Today, Zondervan, and Hislop's The Two Babylons, Loizeaux Brothers, p. 131f.

8 A. Dillmann, Genesis, 1:350, quoted from Unger, p. 48.

9 Cf. the Theological Journal of the Old Testament, Volume 2, p. 672.

10 E. J. Young, The Book of Isaiah, p. 288.

11 Compare Jeremiah 22:28-30 with Matthew 1:1-17; Luke 3:17-38.

12 Warren Wiersbe, Be Loyal, Victor Books, p. 18.

13 J. Dwight Pentecost, The Words and Works of Jesus Christ, Zondervan, p. 67.

14 Stanley D. Toussaint, Behold the King, Multnomah Press, p. 49.

15 James Hope Moulton and George Milligan, The Vocabulary of the Greek Testament, p. 549.

16 See The New International Dictionary of New Testament Theology, edited by Colin Brown, Vol. 2, p. 877.

17 John Walvoord, Matthew, Thy Kingdom Come, p. 22.

To contact the author please visit:

www.jacksonglobalinitiative.com

www.themissionsbase.org

www.facebook.com/apjasonjackson/

Email: Jacqueline.brown@yortransformation.org

About the Author

Recognized as Forbes Finance investment banker, Christian leader, and progressive instructor, Dr. Jason Jackson is a sought after innovative theorist, and transformational guide. Regularly covered by over 150 news outlets, such as CNBC, Boston Globe, and other leading media authorities, Dr. Jackson has earned a distinguished reputation as an agent of restoration to the nations.

Dr. Jackson couples leadership prowess with his wealth of spiritual understanding to deliver transforming teachings that restore and inspire. Compassionate, humorous, and revelatory, Dr. Jackson kindles minds with Christian-based principles of freedom and personal ability. Dr. Jackson is a devoted husband to his wife, Natalie, and father to his children: Nalani, Jessica, and Joshua.

Through his leadership mobilization organization, Jackson Global Initiative, Mr. Jackson serves as a spiritual advisor to government and ministry leaders as well as a diverse group of entrepreneurs. Dr. Jackson takes pride in drawing upon his unique skill set to advance the lives of those within his center of influence by bridging the gap between social, economic, and cultural classes. In addition to his business efforts, Dr. Jackson is serving as the Overseer and Senior Pastor of the Lion's Den Mission Base in Fort Lauderdale, Florida.

JDI

Jackson Development Initiative